THE ROAD TO HALLELUJAH:

Daily Meditations For Advent & Christmas

From The Authors Of *The Immediate Word*

CSS Publishing Company, Inc.
Lima, Ohio

THE ROAD TO HALLELUJAH

FIRST EDITION
Copyright © 2019
by CSS Publishing Co., Inc.

Library of Congress Cataloging-in-Publication Data:
Names: Feldmeyer, Dean, 1951- author.   Title: The road to Hallelujah : daily
meditations for Advent & Christmas /   from the authors of the Immediate word.
Description: First edition. | Lima, Ohio : CSS Publishing Company, Inc.,   2019.
| Mary Austin, for the TIW Team - Dean, Chris,   Bethany, Tom, and George"--
Provided by publisher. Identifiers: LCCN 2019049696 | ISBN 9780788030086 | ISBN
9780788030093   (ebook)   Subjects: LCSH: Advent--Meditations. | Christmas--
Meditations. | Devotional calendars. Classification: LCC BV40 .R625 2019 | DDC
242/.33--dc23   LC record available at https://lccn.loc.gov/2019049696

For more information about CSS Publishing Company resources, visit our website at
www.csspub.com, email us at csr@csspub.com, or call (800) 241-4056.

e-book:
ISBN-13: 978-0-7880-3009-3
ISBN-10: 0-7880-3009-4

ISBN-13: 978-0-7880-3008-6
ISBN-10: 0-7880-3008-6   DIGITALLY PRINTED

Contents

Foreword   7

Introduction   9

The First Sunday of Advent   13
Surprised By Joy By Dean Feldmeyer

The Second Day Of Advent   17
Brand Spanking New By Dean Feldmeyer

The Third Day Of Advent   21
The Bow In The Sky By Dean Feldmeyer

The Fourth Day Of Advent   25
Redeemed By Love By Dean Feldmeyer

The Fifth Day Of Advent   29
A Prayer For Leaders By Dean Feldmeyer

The Sixth Day Of Advent   33
Walk This Way By Dean Feldmeyer

The Seventh Day Of Advent   37
O Come, Emmanuel By Chris Keating

The Eighth Day Of Advent   41
Peaceable Kingdom By Chris Keating

The Ninth Day Of Advent   45
A World Laid Waste By Chris Keating

The Tenth Day Of Advent   49
The Cry Of Comfort By Chris Keating

The Eleventh Day Of Advent   53
Season Of Promise By Chris Keating

The Twelfth Day Of Advent   **57**
Stranger In A Strange Land By Chris Keating

The Thirteenth Day Of Advent   **61**
Jesus' Family Tree By Thomas C. Willadsen

The Fourteenth Day Of Advent   **65**
Exalted And Humbled By Thomas C. Willadsen

The Fifteenth Day Of Advent   **69**
The Road Home By Thomas C. Willadsen

The Sixteenth Day Of Advent   **73**
Hope By Thomas C. Willadsen

The Seventeenth Day Of Advent   **77**
Remember Who You Are; Remember Whose
You Are By Thomas C. Willadsen

The Eighteenth Day Of Advent   **81**
Restored, At Last By Thomas C. Willadsen

The Nineteenth Day Of Advent   **85**
Glamping In The Cedars By Mary Austin

The Twentieth Day Of Advent   **89**
The Bread Of Tears By Mary Austin

The Twenty-First Day Of Advent   **91**
Waiting…, And Waiting By Mary Austin

The Twenty-Second Day Of Advent   **93**
Even Not Deciding Is Deciding By Mary Austin

The Twenty-Third Day Of Advent   **97**
Enough Is Enough By Mary Austin

Nativity Of Our Lord   **99**
Our Story By Mary Austin

The Nativity Of Our Lord   **103**
Let it Go By Bethany Peerbolte

The First Day After Christmas   **107**
A Phrase Of Praise By Bethany Peerbolte

The Second Day After Christmas   **109**
Therefore, Get Wisdom By Bethany Peerbolte

The Third Day After Christmas   **111**
Millstones And Stumbling Blocks
By Bethany Peerbolte

The Fourth Day After Christmas   **113**
Into The Good Place By Bethany Peerbolte

The Fifth Day After Christmas   **117**
Praying, Planning, And Giving
By Bethany Peerbolte

The Sixth Day After Christmas   **119**
(New Year's Eve)
Who Are You? By George Reed

The Seventh Day After Christmas   **123**
(New Year's Day)
Now More Division By George Reed

The Eighth Day After Christmas   **127**
Being Sure By George Reed

The Ninth Day After Christmas   **129**
A Blessing For The Earth By George Reed

The Tenth Day After Christmas   **131**
Standing On Holy Ground By George Reed

The Second Sunday Of Christmas   **133**
Grace Upon Grace By George Reed

About the Authors   **137**

FOREWORD

Advent is the biggest and best gift we receive from the Christian calendar.

In a world excited about accomplishment, and in a season filled with frenzy, Advent invites us to pause. The season summons us into a most unusual activity – actually waiting. As we wait, we hear the wise old prophets again, and listen to Mary's fresh voice, marveling about God's plans. Christmas pageants and choir extravaganzas take a step back, shopping and baking wait their turn, and we settle into God's presence for a time of holy waiting.

In Advent, God invites us to settle in, and to join our ancestors in faith in waiting for the fullness of God's presence in the world. God surely looks at the season's busyness with amusement, knowing that we make ourselves so busy that we miss the gifts of this season. Each time Advent returns, God issues us a holy invitation to push away the things that clamor to be done (today! right now!). God calls us into the deep pause we find in the divine presence, so we can hear the sacred words of promise again.

As you read the season's scriptures again, we hope these reflections will give you a taste of deep hope, all through the season of Advent, into the joy of Christmas and a little beyond. Our prayer is that you find rich grace again this Advent season, in the stillness of prayer and reflection. We are honored to be your companions in this journey of anticipation this year.

Mary Austin, for the TIW Team –
Dean Feldmeyer, Editor
Chris Keating
George Reed
Bethany Peerbolte
Tom Willadsen

INTRODUCTION
O, Little Town Of Bethlehem

There's a Christmas card that comes to mind every time I read or hear those famous lyrics by Episcopal priest Phillips Brooks.

The card shows Joseph standing next to Mary who is sitting on the donkey. They are in silhouette, atop a hill, looking down on this peaceful, quiet little town. The whole thing is tinted in dark blue with some yellow light coming from the windows of some of the houses. White stars are twinkling in the sky. If you look carefully, you can make out the inn and the stable next to it.

And then, my mind says, "Nah. That wasn't the way it was."

First of all, they probably didn't travel alone. It was just too dangerous to do that. They probably traveled in a caravan with other people headed for Bethlehem or other nearby towns.

They probably didn't look as neat and freshly scrubbed as the two on the front of the card do. Bethlehem is about 100 miles from Nazareth. That's about 176,000 steps if you're walking it. Call it a journey of 5-8 days. They probably were hot, dirty, tired, and ready for a bath and a meal.

They certainly didn't arrive at night. No one traveled after dark in those days. They made a camp fire, a big camp fire and they put their stuff in a circle around it with the women and children inside the circle and the men on the outside. The men no doubt took turns standing guard over their fellow travelers.

With all due respect to Father Brooks, the little town of Bethlehem was probably not all that peaceful, either. It was more likely a loud, crowded, raucous mess.

Have you ever been to the Kentucky Derby or the Indianapolis 500?

I grew up in Indianapolis and every year, on the night before Memorial Day, we would drive over to Speedway, the suburb where the track is, and watch the madness. People who wanted to get into the infield for the race camped out in line the night before and they were neither quiet nor peaceful.

It was full on party mode, an Indiana version of Mardi Gras. Drinking, dancing, loud music, and activities continued, from which my mother insisted that we children must avert our eyes and which, most certainly, we did not.

The residents of Speedway, especially those in the blocks immediately adjacent to the track were in full entrepreneurial mode. This would have been 1965 or so and they were charging $50 per night for people to park in their yards. Hamburgers and hotdogs fresh off dad's grill were going for $5 each and bottles of soda and adult beverages were available for a king's ransom.

My brother, Scot and I made a pact that, as soon as we were old enough, we were going to join this wonderful madness but we moved to Cincinnati in 1967, never to return for the race. Too bad. It would have been cool.

Anyway, that's where my imagination takes me when I think of Bethlehem during that census that Augustus ordered, "the first census that took place while Quirinius was governor of Syria." I think of a little town of about 800 people whose population exploded to probably something like 5,000 for the census. And those are real people, not blue tinted, neatly painted, cute people. They were real people in a real town.

The inn? Forget about it. Those room prices were jacked up 200% and were still reserved six months in advance. And the stable? We like to think of it as a straw-strewn shed but I imagine that innkeeper had swept it out and set up rows and rows of cots for his "guests" to rent (special discount for family members).

The streets of that little town were probably alive with revelers. That's what happens when family members who haven't seen each other in a long time get together. There was, no doubt, plenty of drinking, and storytelling and singing and dancing in the streets.

Yeah, I imagine it was quite a blow-out in Bethlehem that year.

And it was into that loud, messy mix that Jesus, our Savior, was born. A real Savior for real people in a real world.

The writing team from *The Immediate Word* (TIW) has kept that image before us as we walked along the road to Bethlehem. And, using that image, we have created what we hope are real meditations for real people who are on a real journey to the Christ child. As we do in our weekly offerings in the *Sermon Suite* we have pressed the lectionary reading for each day through the current events that we find in the newspapers, media broadcasts, and our everyday lives.

We hope this little collection helps you come to Jesus with real faith and return to the world better equipped not just to face Christmas but to face all of life – real life – as well.

Merry Christmas.

The TIW Writing Team --
Dean Feldmeyer, Editor
Mary Austin
Chris Keating
George Reed
Bethany Peerbolte
Tom Willadsen

The First Sunday of Advent

Surprised By Joy
By Dean Feldmeyer

Matthew 24:36-42

> *"But about that day and hour no one knows, neither the angels of heaven, nor the Son, but only the Father. For as the days of Noah were, so will be the coming of the Son of Man. For as in those days before the flood they were eating and drinking, marrying and giving in marriage, until the day Noah entered the ark, and they knew nothing until the flood came and swept them all away, so too will be the coming of the Son of Man. Then two will be in the field; one will be taken and one will be left. "Two women will be grinding meal together; one will be taken and one will be left. Keep awake therefore, for you do not know on what day your Lord is coming."*

IN THE WORD

We begin the Advent season, the season of self-examination, of repentance, of waiting, of watching, and of expecting with a warning from Matthew: Jesus is coming and if we are not vigilant, we will miss him.

He is coming in unexpected ways and times and places. He is coming when we least expect it.

His coming is not just limited to Christmas morning. He is given to us everywhere and always but often in ways and at times we don't expect.

So, watch!

13

IN THE WORLD

It was in the very heart of the Christmas season and I was wrapping up my day in the grocery store... again. Never a day passed, it seemed, that I didn't have to stop at the grocery for something. I felt like I was on a first name basis with the guy behind the meat counter.

This time I was supposed to pick up something for supper. Something quick and easy with not a lot of clean-up... and, oh, something cheap, too - and healthy.

I was tired.

The store was hot and crowded.

I wanted all these people to go away and let me get my rotisserie chicken and cottage cheese and go home. Then, for all I cared, they could have full run of the place until Christmas.

I looked around and it seemed that everyone in the place looked and felt exactly the way I did: hot, tired, impatient, petulant, and on the verge of a meltdown.

And then, without warning, something happened that lifted me out of my recalcitrant revelry. Nothing big or explosive, nothing earth shattering or world changing or mind blowing. On the contrary, it was a thing so simple, so small, so innocently lovely that, had I not been in precisely the right place at the right time, I might have missed it.

It was, simply, laughter – the pure, sweet, innocent, laughter of a child. And, like the pied piper's song, it so captivated me that I had to follow the sound of it to see its source.

He was maybe five or six years old.

His heavy winter coat was hanging off his shoulders, threatening to fall to the floor, his mittens clipped to each sleeve and dangling like caught fish.

His face was flushed red and his hair matted with perspiration.

And he was laughing - laughing without a care in the world.

The store was running a sale on DVD's and they had set up a monitor showing the DreamWorks favorite, *Madagascar*. The sound was turned down so we could hardly hear it but this little boy, this audience of one had obviously seen the movie before and he was laughing at every gag, hearing the dialogue in his mind's ear as he watched.

He was laughing, and his laughter was like a bell, sweet and pure, innocent, and full of love and life, calling to me, summoning me to come and see. It was contagious. It infected everyone who walked by. We adults, so sour and so tired of the season could not help but smile and nod to each other as we passed through the shower of mirth which he poured over us so freely, as a gift.

For he had surprised us with joy and made us forget our doubt and our cynicism, our discomforts and dissatisfactions and remember if only for an hour, that this, this kind of joy, this kind of laughter is what awaits us with the coming of the Christ child.

THINK ABOUT

When have you been surprised by contagious joy? Did you recognize it as a Christ moment?

When have you missed a Christ moment and only recognized it in retrospect?

How might we create a Christ moment for others by surprising them with our joy?

PRAYER

Awaken us, Lord, to the bright and lovely promise of your son, and open our hearts to the surprising joy that he promises to brings us, not just on Christmas, but every day. Amen.

The Second Day Of Advent

Brand Spanking New
By Dean Feldmeyer

Romans 6: 1-4

What then are we to say? Should we continue in sin in order that grace may abound? By no means! How can we who died to sin go on living in it? Do you not know that all of us who have been baptized into Christ Jesus were baptized into his death? Therefore we have been buried with him by baptism into death, so that, just as Christ was raised from the dead by the glory of the Father, so we too might walk in newness of life.

IN THE WORD
Jesus makes all things new. Even us!

In a few weeks we will celebrate his birth by joining him in his life and, yes, in his death and in his resurrection. As we progress along this journey with our Savior we will not necessarily be changed but we will be transformed. We will see and experience life differently than we have before.

The life we live will be new life and we who live it will be brand spanking new people.

IN THE WORLD
Old Methodist Joke --

Question: How many Methodists does it take to change a lightbulb?

Answer: Change? Change? You can't change that lightbulb! My grandmother gave that lightbulb to the church!

When I was sixteen years old, preparing for my junior year in high school, my father came home and announced that we were moving from Indianapolis, where I had spent my entire sixteen years, to Cincinnati where I knew no one and about which I knew nothing.

I was not excited by the promise of this move.

I was active in youth fellowship at my church and in the district youth fellowship as well. I was a starter on the football team and a solid second stringer on the basketball team. I sang in the concert choir and played baritone in the band.

I was a popular class clown at school, I was loved in my church, and, perhaps most importantly of all, I had a girlfriend.

One day, when I was feeling particularly sorry for myself, my mother asked me how I was doing, handling the news of the move and all. I was honest with her. I hated it.

Mom had a tough childhood.

Her dad was an alcoholic who suffered from a wanderlust that bordered on mental illness. In twelve years, she had gone to eight schools in seven different towns and this during the Great Depression. She shared something she had learned from all those moves.

"When you move," she said, "You start with a clean slate. You can completely reinvent yourself. You can be anyone you want to be. Don't be too quick to make friends. Take your time. Get to know people and let them get to know the real you."

For one of the few times in my life, I took my parent's advice.

I had been a class clown in Indianapolis, always quick with a joke, a prank, or a goofy comeback. I prayed and asked for God's help as I decided that in Cincinnati I would be more serious. Not morose, but a little more contemplative and thoughtful.

And it worked. With God's help, I embraced the change being thrust upon me and used it as an opportunity to change who I was.

In two years, before I graduated, I was elected president of the senior class, vice president of the student council, and section leader in the band. I was president of the youth fellowship at church and delegate to the conference youth council. I was voted most likely to succeed in the senior class and given an award for outstanding citizenship from the local Lion's Club.

With God's help, I changed myself into a new person.

This, said Paul to the Romans, is the kind of thing we can expect if we are willing to turn our lives over to Jesus Christ – positive change, transformation, growth, development into a brand spanking new person.

THINK ABOUT
What changes have you feared only to discover that they were actually beneficial?

If a change is being offered to you, how might you pray for God's help in navigating it so you can grow and learn through it.

PRAYER
Holy one, help me to ride the changes that come to me so that, in them, I might be made new for your sake and the sake of your kingdom. In Jesus' holy name. Amen.

The Third Day Of Advent

The Bow In The Sky
By Dean Feldmeyer

Genesis 9: 12 - 17

> *God said, "This is the sign of the covenant that I
> make between me and you and every living creature
> that is with you, for all future generations: I have set
> my bow in the clouds, and it shall be a sign of the
> covenant between me and the earth. When I bring
> clouds over the earth and the bow is seen in the clouds,
> I will remember my covenant that is between me and
> you and every living creature of all flesh; and the
> waters shall never again become a flood to destroy all
> flesh. When the bow is in the clouds, I will see it and
> remember the everlasting covenant between God and
> every living creature of all flesh that is on the earth."
> God said to Noah, "This is the sign of the covenant that
> I have established between me and all flesh that is on
> the earth."*

IN THE WORD
In today's passage from Genesis we are reminded that God
makes promises and keeps them. God is faithful and so are we
called to be faithful in the way we make and keep our promises.

IN THE WORLD
My mother's father had many faults and difficulties. He was
an alcoholic and, today, he would almost surely be diagnosed as
bipolar. But he also had his share of strengths, one of which was
a solid value system based on his Christian upbringing.

This story about him may be apocryphal but it has been told in my family for years as a parable about the value of promise keeping:

During World War II it was nearly impossible to buy a new car as all of the resources required to build them were being used in the war effort. Steel for the body, rubber for the tires, and glass for the windows were all in short supply. And even if you could buy a car, gas and oil were severely rationed so most people's driving was limited to only essential trips.

After the war, however, things changed and almost instantly.

Within a few weeks, automobile dealerships were being flooded with customers and my grandfather, Howard Clark, was among them.

It had been a long time since he bought a new car and the $1,100 - $1,400 average price tag on a new car in 1946 was a lot of money, so he was determined to make a wise decision that would require him to look at what was being offered by both Ford and General Motors – the only two dealerships in the small, Indiana town where my family lived.

He set out on his journey on a Saturday morning and went first to the Ford dealership where he looked at all the cars that were or would shortly be available. He saw one he liked but, he told the salesman, he really thought he should look at what General Motors had to offer as well.

The salesman said he certainly understood, but Howard knew that this man was being paid on a commission basis so he told him, "If I decide on the Ford, I'll come back here and buy it from you."

He went to the GM dealership and saw some cars there that he liked as well but, he said, that the salesman was kind of a "wheeler-dealer" type of guy that put him off. Finally, he told the wheeler-dealer that he had decided on the Ford but the flashy salesman was not to be undone. He asked Howard what model he was going to buy and when my grandfather told him, the salesman winked, smiled, and nudged Howard's shoulder. "I know a guy in [the county seat] that owns a Ford dealership. I can get you that car $100 dollars cheaper than the guy here in our town."

My grandfather said that he was sorely tempted. $100 was nearly 10% of the entire price of the car but, he said, "I gave that salesman at the Ford dealership my word, and I figured my word was worth a heck of a lot more than $100."

THINK ABOUT

Have you ever experienced having an important promise to you broken? How did it feel? How do you show people that the promises you make are important?

What are some of God's promises to us in which you find comfort?

PRAYER

We give you thanks, Lord, for the promises you have given to us, the promises you have kept. We especially thank you for the promise of love and forgiveness which you have made to us in your son, Jesus Christ, whose birth we will soon celebrate. Amen.

The Fourth Day Of Advent

Redeemed By Love
By Dean Feldmeyer

Isaiah 54:4-8

> *Do not fear, for you will not be ashamed; do not be discouraged, for you will not suffer disgrace;*
> *for you will forget the shame of your youth, and the disgrace of your widowhood you will remember no more. For your maker is your husband, the Lord of hosts is his name; the Holy One of Israel is your Redeemer, the God of the whole earth he is called.*
> *For the Lord has called you like a wife forsaken and grieved in spirit, like the wife of a man's youth when she is cast off, says your God. For a brief moment I abandoned you, but with great compassion I will gather you. In overflowing wrath for a moment I hid my face from you, but with everlasting love I will have compassion on you, says the Lord, your Redeemer.*
> *This is like the days of Noah to me: Just as I swore that the waters of Noah would never again go over the earth,*
> *so I have sworn that I will not be angry with you and will not rebuke you. For the mountains may depart and the hills be removed, but my steadfast love shall not depart from you, and my covenant of peace shall not be removed, says the Lord, who has compassion on you.*

IN THE WORD

Isaiah spoke of God's desire to bring the children of Israel back to their homeland from their captivity in Babylon and he used the metaphor of a husband who cast off his unfaithful wife but then, because of his great love and grace, forgave her and returned to her to accept her, once again, as his beloved.

The double theme for this day is God's grace and forgiveness as they come to us in Jesus Christ.

IN THE WORLD

What was rejected and lost is saved and redeemed.

Nearly fifty years ago, when my wife and I were first married, we were poor. Really poor. She was working as a registered nurse and I was struggling to finish grad school and we were constantly strapped for cash.

In those days most stores would pay two cents for an empty, glass soda pop bottle and we would spend many weekends scouring the ditches and roadsides for empties that we could take home, clean, and redeem at our local super market.

For help, we would recruit my two younger brothers to join us in our searches by promising them that any money we made we would use to do something fun and we would take them with us. Over a couple of years our pop-bottle-missions made enough money for us to take Ben and Brian to the state fair, to Cincinnati's Coney Island, fishing at a local state park, and more late nights at the drive-in movies than I can count from memory.

The thing that made all this possible was that two cents was such a small amount.

To most people two cents was just not enough to make them care about saving their pop bottle and redeeming it. Two-cent pop bottles were, to them, worthless, especially if they were lying in a ditch, covered with mud and... whatever.

But we didn't see the mud and whatever. We didn't see empty, worthless pop bottles. Every time we found one my brothers would send up a shout of glee because what they saw in that nasty old bottle was the state fair, and the fishing lake, and the drive-in movie.

Those bottles had value.

We restored them and redeemed them.

And so it is that when God looks upon us, God does not see the muck and grime that has spoiled our appearance, the separation and estrangement, the unfaithfulness, the meanness and pettiness that has hurt the feelings of those we love.

No, what God sees is the potential within us, the potential for love and redemption, the potential for kindness and grace and peace and renewel.

God sent Jesus Christ to reach down and pull us out of the muddy ditch into which we have thrown our lives and clean us up and redeem us so that we can do good in the world, good that is far better than the state fair, and the fishing trips, and the drive-in movies.

Even though those were pretty good, too.

THINK ABOUT

Have you ever felt that you were redeemed or were being redeemed by God?

From what have you been redeemed?

Have you ever participated in the redemption of another? What did that feel like? Would you do it again?

PRAYER

We give you thanks and praise, O God, that you have given us your son, Jesus Christ, who pulls us out of our sin, separation, and despair, washes the grime from our lives, and redeems us for greater, more authentic living. And it is in his name that we pray this prayer. Amen.

The Fifth Day Of Advent

A Prayer For Leaders
By Dean Feldmeyer

Psalm 72: 1-7

> *Give the king your justice, O God, and your*
> *righteousness to a king's son. May he judge your people*
> *with righteousness, and your poor with justice. May the*
> *mountains yield prosperity for the people, and the hills,*
> *in righteousness. May he defend the cause of the poor*
> *of the people, give deliverance to the needy, and crush*
> *the oppressor. May he live while the sun endures, and as*
> *long as the moon, throughout all generations. May he*
> *be like rain that falls on the mown grass, like showers*
> *that water the earth. In his days may righteousness*
> *flourish and peace abound, until the moon is no more.*

IN THE WORD

Psalm 72 is both a prayer for the king and an injunction
to the king. Compare the NIV and the NRSV (above), both of
which are appropriate translations and we see that both prayer
and injunction are apparent. The NIV says that if God will bless
the king the king will do thus-and-so. The NRSV prays for the
king so that he will do thus-and-so.

What is this thus-and-so the king is to do? Why, justice and
righteousness, certainly. See how often those two words are
repeated in the seven verses above. And, for the psalmist, justice
and righteousness have mostly to do with how we treat the poor
(vs. 4).

Finally, the psalmist concludes that if the king is committed to the cause of justice and righteousness, especially for the poor, then the result will be "shalom" (peace) for the whole nation.

That this prayer was still used after the monarchy ended in Israel shows that it applied not just to kings but to leaders of all sorts. It contains both prayers and admonitions for politicians, bosses, teachers, preachers, and all those who would aspire to lead others.

IN THE WORLD

I'm old enough to remember when the President Lyndon Johnson declared a "War on Poverty" in his first state of the Union address.

In 2004, on the fortieth anniversary of that declaration, National Public Radio made this observation about President Johnson's massive program:

"Making poverty a national concern set in motion a series of bills and acts, creating programs such as Head Start, food stamps, work study, Medicare and Medicaid, which still exist today. The programs initiated under Johnson brought about real results, reducing rates of poverty and improving living standards for America's poor.

"But the poverty rate has remained steady since the 1970s and today, Americans have allowed poverty to fall off the national agenda."[1]

Even with all those successes, President Johnson's War on Poverty was only a measured blessing.

But a measured blessing was better than no blessing at all. The fact that we made the attempt to address the fact that nearly one in every five Americans lived in poverty at that time is remarkable. It is not unlike what Winston Churchill reportedly said about dogs dancing on their hind legs: "It is not that they do it well that please us, but that they do it at all."

We don't hear many politicians talking about the plight of the poor, these days.

The poor are not a very profitable voting block. They tend to not show up at the polls. They certainly don't contribute heavily to campaigns and they don't create political action committees or pac-funds.

1 https://www.npr.org/templates/story/story.php?storyId=1589660

If the poor are mentioned at all it is often to berate them and to blame them for their plight as though it is their own fault. At the very best they are sometimes thrown a bone in the form of a higher minimum wage, sometimes one that is even large enough to support a family.

But mostly, political points these days are scored by pandering to the middle class. They vote and, sometimes, they throw a few bucks into a campaign coffer.

Then there are the rich. The wealthy are the king makers. And, thanks to Citizens United, they can find a seemingly endless number of legal ways to contribute millions of dollars to political campaigns creating, debts of gratitude between them and the politicians they support.

In such a political climate the words of Psalm 72 ring loudly in our hearts and minds.

The psalmist prays for the king and, later, other leaders who are symbolized in the word "king," so that they will have the strength and the vision to lead with justice and righteousness for the poor.

Perhaps what we're talking about, here, is more than throwing a handful of change into the red kettle at Christmas time. Perhaps what we're talking about is attacking poverty at the systemic level, at its root wherever people are kept poor because they make better, more dependent, more docile employees. Perhaps what the psalmist is praying for is a system government that lifts up those who are the most desperate and hopeless and leaders who are bright enough and strong enough to lead such a system.

THINK ABOUT

There's nothing wrong with throwing some bucks into the red kettle, but what would it look like to also support a ministry that works at defeating the need for red kettles?

Who profits from keeping the poor, poor? How can we fight such a system?

How can we teach our children that there is more to justice and righteousness than being generous at Christmastime?

PRAYER (Psalm 72: 1-4 paraphrase)

Give our leaders your justice, O God, and your righteousness to all who would lead us.

May they lead your people with righteousness, and treat those who are poor with justice.

May our mountains of wealth yield prosperity for all the people, and may the hills of profit conduct their business with righteousness.

May every leader, in government, in business, in education, in church, defend the cause of the poor,

And give deliverance to those whose need is genuine, and crush the aspirations of those who use the needy for their own gain. Amen.

The Sixth Day Of Advent

Walk This Way
By Dean Feldmeyer

Isaiah 30:19-22

> *Truly, O people in Zion, inhabitants of Jerusalem, you shall weep no more. He will surely be gracious to you at the sound of your cry; when he hears it, he will answer you. Though the Lord may give you the bread of adversity and the water of affliction, yet your Teacher will not hide himself any more, but your eyes shall see your Teacher. And when you turn to the right or when you turn to the left, your ears shall hear a word behind you, saying, "This is the way; walk in it." Then you will defile your silver-covered idols and your gold-plated images. You will scatter them like filthy rags; you will say to them, "Away with you!"*

IN THE WORD

Isaiah offered a word of encouragement to the children of Israel. Yes, he said, you have experienced the full consequences of your infidelity and your apostasy and your idolatry, but that period of consequence will eventually end.

It will be replaced by a time when YHWH puts on the teacher's cap and gown and walks with you through your days and nights. God will be with you to inform and instruct you and when that happens you will finally realize how silly and worthless are the trinkets and toys of this world. You will toss them away like trash, like filthy rags, and you will be content to walk with the Lord.

About 1,000 years later, Christians would see in this passage the reflection of Jesus Christ.

In the season of Advent we prepare for the arrival of Emmanuel, God-with-us, in the person of Jesus Christ. Isaiah reminds us that one of the ways that God is with us is as a teacher.

IN THE WORLD

Five minutes for a GTA (Graduate Teaching Assistant).
Ten minutes for a Master's Degree.
Fifteen minutes for a Ph.D.

When I was a college student, that was the unwritten rule about how long you wait for a professor who is running late. If they didn't show up for class in the allotted time you were allowed to leave.

I don't know who made up that rule. Certainly not the professors or instructors. I never saw it written down anywhere but everyone seemed to be absolutely sure that it was a hard and fast rule and it applied to every situation, because if you want to learn, really learn, you need a teacher. You need a flesh and blood human being to show you and explain to you and answer your questions. You can get some things from a book and some things from a video or a web page but if you're really serious about the process of learning you'll go out and find a teacher.

My mom taught me to cook, not by giving me a cookbook but by showing me. I would sit on a stool in the kitchen and tell her how my day went while she cooked supper and she would explain to me what she was doing and why.

Later, she would suggest that I try it while she watched and made corrections and suggestions.

We started with frying an egg and, over the years, we moved up from there.

She knew, instinctively, the pedagogical method: I do it while you watch. We do it together. You do it while I watch. You do it alone.

As we make our way through Advent we would do well to think of God, especially as God comes to us in Jesus Christ, not just as the holy one of Israel but as our pedagogue and teacher.

THINK ABOUT

Who were the teachers that taught you the important things, small and large? Say their names out loud and give thanks for them.

Who are you teaching? Who have you taken under your wing? Who are you bringing into the house of the Lord?

Who will look back and name your name when asked, "Who taught you?"

PRAYER

I give you thanks, good Lord, for all the teachers in my life who sacrificed of themselves so that I could learn and grow and live. And especially I thank you for the great teacher, Jesus Christ, who taught me about grace, even grace from a cross. So it is in his name that I pray. Amen.

The Seventh Day Of Advent

O Come, Emmanuel
By Chris Keating

Isaiah 40:1-11

> *Comfort, O comfort my people, says your God.*
> *Speak tenderly to Jerusalem, and cry to her that she has*
> *served her term, that her penalty is paid, that she has*
> *received from the LORD's hand double for all her sins...*

IN THE WORD

A little boy leans forward to light the Advent candles and somehow lights the candles without engulfing the entire wreath in flames. His mother breathes a sigh of relief, and the liturgist begins the call to worship. The boy handles the long candle lighter as if it were a Jedi lightsaber and he was a Star Wars apprentice. As the choir begins singing "O Come, O Come Emmanuel," the pint-sized Padawan makes his retreat. Advent has come, the Lord is at hand, and now is the time to prepare.

A curious feeling of comfort mixed with anticipation is expressed in their voices. *Veni, veni,* Emmanuel.

It is the second week of Advent, and all is bright with imagination, dreams of peace, and words of comfort. Second Isaiah's words of comfort, so familiar to many, ring in our ears. The prophet delivered promises of soothing relief to those whose hearts have been crushed, and whose lives are as withered as drying desert grass.

Scholars point to the shift in tone and vocabulary in Isaiah 40-55 as indicators that these chapters are the work of another writer often referred to as "Second Isaiah" or "Deutero-Isaiah." The expected exile had happened. Lives have been disrupted and the conquest of Israel's hopes, dreams, and places of worship have been completed.

37

The exile was never directly addressed, but rather assumed. The event hung in the air like a tragedy so severe no words can adequately describe it. Like nine-year-old 9-11 survivor Oscar Schell in Jonathan Safran Foer's novel *Extremely Loud and Incredibly Close*, Israel was tormented by the horrible, awful experiences of abandonment and severed hope.

Until, however, a voice began to cry out. "Get ready! Make room for the coming of the Lord!" Get rid of all the obstacles and clear a pathway for the one who will lead the return to Zion. Climb up to a high place and see it for yourself: Yahweh is returning with a paradoxical mixture of both strength and gentleness.

The image is challenging. The people have sinned, and God's judgment has been executed. At the same time, it appeared that Yahweh had heard the cries of those long oppressed. It was enough.

The scripture confirms this challenging mix of images. The flower withers and fades, but the word of the Lord stands forever. God comes with might and strength, but will feed the flock like a gentle shepherd, guiding the stray lambs back to their mother's bosom.

Prepare. Hope. Pray. It's a lot for a young Padawan acolyte or even his mother to absorb. But like Israel in exile, they cling to the hope. *Veni, veni,* Emmanuel.

IN THE WORLD

Second Isaiah's words are a reminder that, even for God, timing is everything. The prophet called the people to turn from their laments into an active stance of preparing. Clear out the obstacles, get rid of the debris, haul off all that will get in the way. God is coming.

These words are meant for our comfort, and are a reminder of the sort of preparations we ought to be undertaking during Advent. Serious Christmas planners advise beginning holiday planning early — as in August or September. Last year we met a professional designer at a Christmas party who admitted that he had begun decorating his yard on a humid August morning.

By December, the pros say, our check lists should be completed, with only bits and pieces remaining. Refreshing greenery and adjusting table linens are the tasks at hand, not hauling boxes of ornaments down from the attic. If you're just starting to prepare, why, you might be a little too late.

Meanwhile, John the Baptist is busy preparing in different ways. In the wilderness, John is offering the baptism of repentance, a message that this is perhaps the most important way to prepare for God's coming. "Prepare yourselves," he preaches. "Not by acting busy, but by turning around, and living with hope."

Prepare. Hope. Pray. *Veni, veni,* Emmanuel.

THINK ABOUT

In a month filled with preparations, how are you preparing yourself spiritually for Christmas?

What sort of Advent preparations might help you center yourself in grace, peace, and joy instead of the non-stop frantic pace so often experienced during the holidays?

PRAYER

Loving God, you hear our cries and promise us comfort. As we await the coming of your son, help us to clear away the obstacles which keep us from fully participating in the promise of your reign. Amen.

The Eighth Day Of Advent

Peaceable Kingdom
By Chris Keating

Isaiah 11:1-3,6-7, 9

> *A shoot shall come out from the stump of Jesse,*
> *and a branch shall grow out of his roots. The spirit of*
> *the Lord shall rest on him, the spirit of wisdom and*
> *understanding, the spirit of counsel and might, the*
> *spirit of knowledge and the fear of the Lord. His delight*
> *shall be in the fear of the Lord.... The wolf shall live*
> *with the lamb, the leopard shall lie down with the kid,*
> *the calf and the lion and the fatling together, and a little*
> *child shall lead them. The cow and the bear shall graze,*
> *their young shall lie down together; and the lion shall*
> *eat straw like the ox... They will not hurt or destroy on*
> *all my holy mountain; for the earth will be full of the*
> *knowledge of the Lord as the waters cover the sea.*

IN THE WORD

Isaiah's prophetic image of the kingdom of peace is as iconic as it is ironic. At first blush, the prophet's words seem improbable, if not unsafe. The passage is full of unlikely events, beginning with new life sprouting out of a lifeless stump. The branch arose from the smoldering ruins of failure, likely a reference to the King David's failed offspring. Then the branch was replaced by even more incongruous pairings: a wolf befriending a lamb, a leopard resting next to a young goat. Predator and prey exist together.

"But wait," Isaiah said, "there's more!" A young child will lead this improbable grouping in royal processional of sorts. Moreover, it shall be the sort of oddball kingdom where carnivores go vegan and enemies become kin. Even helpless infants will be able to play near the dens of venomous snakes. All creation will be transformed. There will be no need for the ever-watchful "Elf on a Shelf," because no one will ever be naughty.

Sandwiched between these paragraphs is a description of the new ruler Isaiah envisioned for Israel. The new king would be anointed with the spirit of Yahweh. The barrenness of the previous dynasty would yield a ruler who would be given the "spirit of wisdom and understanding," and whose "delight shall be in the fear of the Lord." The king would act with justice and would safeguard the helpless, poor, and marginalized.

Early generations of Christians read these verses and nodded their heads in agreement. All of this had been fulfilled, they believed, by Jesus. Yet first let the power intended for its original audience speak. Listen to the text as it captures the longing for the arrival of a king who will bring justice and transformation to the social order.

Such a ruler will fulfill the prayer of Psalm 72 by judging with righteousness, defending the poor, and ruling with God's justice.

IN THE WORLD

As the second week of Advent dawns, it's not likely there is much in our life which is either peaceful or tranquil. Isaiah's images of a world at peace works well on Christmas cards and Advent calendars, but bears little resemblance to the frantic holiday pace most of us know. While we may wish for the beauty and majesty of Edward Hicks' painting *Peaceable Kingdom*, the real-world of December is chaotic and disruptive. Think *National Lampoon's Christmas Vacation*, and Clark Griswold's bumbling efforts to achieve the perfect holiday.

But it isn't just our own personal lives. Our world is far from peaceful. It is cluttered by pollution and filled with injustice to the poor. Floods and storms pummel those with the fewest resources. Headlines of terror attacks and mass shootings crawl across television screens. Our phones vibrate with alerts about the latest corruption and scandals. Forget about cows and bears sharing a cup of Christmas tea. In our version of the world, they're battling it out on Twitter and Facebook, or yelling at each other in Congress. And while no parent could imagine infants playing with deadly snakes, we know very little about the toxins present in the water they drink. Our world is a hot mess.

All creation yearns for the coming of one who will bring justice and peace. We long for the equity God will bring; we dream of the righteousness that will draw us in close like a belt. We're not quite ready to plan lock-ins for lions and lambs, but we can allow Isaiah's words to calm the chaos within us. We can engage in the practices of Advent — lighting candles, setting up nativity scenes, praying for peace. It's time to prepare our hearts for the coming the Lord, while also trying to figure out a menu which will be pleasing to both the calves and lions in our lives.

THINK ABOUT

Where do you see signs of God's incomparable peace arising this Advent?

For what does your spirit long this week?

What simple steps can you take this week to convey care for creation?

PRAYER

Lord, grant us the unfailing encouragement and steadfastness of your Spirit in these days of Advent, so that we live in harmony with each other and eagerly await the coming of your son. Amen.

The Ninth Day Of Advent

A World Laid Waste

By Chris Keating

Isaiah 24:1-16a

*See, the LORD is going to lay waste the earth
and devastate it; he will ruin its face and scatter
its inhabitants — it will be the same for priest as
for people, for the master as for his servant, for the
mistress as for her servant, for seller as for buyer,
for borrower as for lender, for debtor as for creditor.
The earth will be completely laid waste and totally
plundered. The LORD has spoken this word. The earth
dries up and withers, the world languishes and withers,
the heavens languish with the earth. The earth is defiled
by its people; they have disobeyed the laws, violated the
statutes and broken the everlasting covenant. Therefore
a curse consumes the earth; its people must bear their
guilt. Therefore earth's inhabitants are burned up, and
very few are left. The new wine dries up and the vine
withers; all the merrymakers groan. The joyful timbrels
are stilled, the noise of the revelers has stopped, the
joyful harp is silent. No longer do they drink wine with
a song; the beer is bitter to its drinkers. The ruined city
lies desolate; the entrance to every house is barred. In
the streets they cry out for wine; all joy turns to gloom,
all joyful sounds are banished from the earth. The city
is left in ruins, its gate is battered to pieces. So will it be
on the earth and among the nations, as when an olive
tree is beaten, or as when gleanings are left after the*

grape harvest. They raise their voices, they shout for joy; from the west they acclaim the LORD's majesty. Therefore in the east give glory to the LORD; exalt the name of the LORD, the God of Israel, in the islands of the sea. From the ends of the earth we hear singing: "Glory to the Righteous One."

IN THE WORD

At first blush, there is little comfort and joy in today's readings. Isaiah's vision of creation laid waste by pollution feels as welcoming as a Christmas tree stripped of lights and tinsel. The lectionary offers us more Scrooge than Cratchit, and more Grinch than the sweet little Cindy-Loo Who.

We're awakened this Advent Monday by the prophet's call to see the languishing world, and to join in eagerly anticipating the one who brings salvation. The radio may be blaring Wham's "Last Christmas," but on this Advent Monday, the prophet is calling us to see a world filled with devastation. God's judgment awaits.

Isaiah surveys the polluted landscape of Israel, decrying the sinfulness of humanity that has led to joylessness and treachery. Some commentators see allusions to the story of Noah in Isaiah 24, with the surface of the earth being twisted and all creation laid waste. God's ways have been rejected and the law ignored. Human sinfulness has resulted in a twisted, polluted, and stinking moral mess. Isaiah was taking aim at the moral pollution of his time, of course, but there is a connection to our contemporary environmental concerns which should not escape our attention.

Isaiah believed Israel's failure to maintain covenant faithfulness had created waves of joylessness malaise that mirrored the brokenness of creation. "The mirth of the timbrels is stilled, the noise of the jubilant has ceased." (Is. 24:8). In this time of destruction and hopelessness, however, the prophet leans forward in hopes of hearing the faintest sounds of praise.

Similarly, Paul's admonitions to the Thessalonians included instructions about faithfulness in a time of apocalyptic terror. He expressed his desire to be with them and was effusive in his remembrance of their faithfulness. The tone shifted a bit in chapter four. To withstand the ordeals that were to come, Paul called the church to abstain from impure activities and to seek pathways of holiness. Paul urged the church to live in ways that were pleasing to God, and to increase in faithfulness.

IN THE WORLD

It's not hard to look and see places where human sinfulness and greed have laid waste to the earth and despoiled its beauty. We have poked holes in the atmosphere. Our excess plastic has ended up in the ocean, where an island three times the size of France now floats between California and Hawaii. Inland flooding has increased in recent years, one of the indicators of how extreme weather caused by climate change will continue to impact the world.

The data of despair is as numbing as it is global. Climate change has accelerated the rate of ice melt in Antarctica, leaving large portions of the continent unstable. Wildfires have plagued western regions, with millions impacted. Deforestation, pollution, and climate change have hastened the extinction of various species, resulting in what many scientists believe is the sixth mass extinction.

"The mirth of the timbrels is stilled, the noise of the jubilant has ceased." (Is 24:8) Isaiah's eco-theology speaks to the despair many feel today.

Yet God's word is rooted in hope. Isaiah heard the distant shouts of joy, and trusted that the Lord would come. Paul pointed to the possibilities of individual choices as pathways to holiness. In our world today, creation shouts for joy when even a few persons choose pathways of greater sustainability. Rob Shumaker, president of the Indianapolis Zoo, has said he has seen how the efforts of a single person have resulted in saving an endangered species. Individuals, said Shumaker, have more power than they think.

As Paul reminded us, each one knows how to control our own actions.

THINK ABOUT

What are simple steps you can take this Advent to reduce, reuse, and recycle?

Where can you shop locally for Christmas gifts in order to reduce carbon emissions?

What practices can your church adopt to encourage greater environmental awareness?

PRAYER

Help us to listen to the cries of the earth, O Lord, as it shouts out in pain and struggle. Give us courage in making faithful decisions and let us trust in your steadfast provision so that all generations may know and delight in the gift of your creation. Amen.

The Tenth Day Of Advent

The Cry Of Comfort

By Chris Keating

Isaiah 41:14-20

Do not fear, you worm Jacob, you insect[a] Israel!
I will help you, says the Lord; your Redeemer is the
Holy One of Israel. Now, I will make of you a threshing
sledge, sharp, new, and having teeth; you shall thresh
the mountains and crush them, and you shall make the
hills like chaff. You shall winnow them and the wind
shall carry them away, and the tempest shall scatter
them. Then you shall rejoice in the Lord; in the Holy
One of Israel you shall glory. When the poor and
needy seek water, and there is none, and their tongue is
parched with thirst, I the Lord will answer them, I the
God of Israel will not forsake them. I will open rivers
on the bare heights,[h] and fountains in the midst of
the valleys; I will make the wilderness a pool of water,
and the dry land springs of water. I will put in the
wilderness the cedar, the acacia, the myrtle, and the
olive; I will set in the desert the cypress, the plane and
the pine together, so that all may see and know, all may
consider and understand, that the hand of the Lord has
done this, the Holy One of Israel has created it.

Romans 15:18

For I will not venture to speak of anything except
what Christ has accomplished through me to win

obedience from the Gentiles, by word and deed, by the
power of signs and wonders, by the power of the Spirit
of God...

IN THE WORD

As the cold of winter settles around us, the cry of the prophet brings comfort and the reassuring promise of God's presence. News of that promise could not have come any sooner. On Sunday, we watched as the second candle of Advent was lit, perhaps singing the favorite Advent lyrics, "Comfort, comfort, now my people; tell of peace so says our God." ("Comfort, Comfort, Now My People," text by Johannes Olearius, 1671, in the public domain.) The cry of comfort is what we long to hear in our Advent waiting.

The prophet described to us as "Second Isaiah" wrote of God's comfort and reconciliation during the final years of the Babylonian exile around 540 BCE. Those who had been devastated by the destruction of Jerusalem longed for the tender assurance of God's deliverance and grace. The prophet declares words of hope to people shattered by despair. In chapter 41, judgment is proclaimed to the nations, but Israel is told to hold fast to God's promise. "For I, the Lord your God, hold your right hand; it is I who say to you, 'Do not fear, I will help you.'"

Beginning at verse 41, this assurance is linked to words commonly associated with prayers of lamentation. Israel is called a "worm," or "insect," underscoring the lowly position and hopelessness of the people. Against the backdrop of despair comes the steady refrain of hope: "Do not fear," "I will help you," "you shall rejoice," "you shall glory." Israel's assurance, so long awaited, shall come. Those who thirst for the taste of clear, clean water shall discover the assurance of God. These lines reverberate with hope and broadcast the promise of faith. Expectations are building that hearts will soon be healed. Soon, "all may consider and understand that the hand of the Lord has done this." Soon, and very soon.

IN THE WORLD

Our lives are so full at Advent it is hard imagining what it would be like to be depleted. It seems there is always something to do – shopping, decorating, cooking – or places to go – concerts, pageants, parties. Unlike those to whom Second Isaiah sought to comfort, our lives are anything but barren.

Or so it may seem.

In truth, all that glitters may not be golden. For many, the brightness of the holidays is dimmed by loss, grief or depression. Even our holiday busyness may be a façade which covers deeper levels of struggle. Surrounded by abundance, we may still feel empty.

Many, for example, will resonate with Isaiah's pronouncement to the poverty stricken: "When the poor and needy seek water, and there is none, and their tongue is parched with thirst, I the Lord will answer them." It's been more than five years since families in Flint, Michigan, learned their drinking water was toxic. While progress has been made, there are many in Flint who still have poisoned water supplies. Across America, more than 1.6 million persons lack access to clean water. Outdated infrastructure will only make those numbers rise. In a land of plenty, there is still plenty of thirst.

Isaiah's words bring comfort to the despairing. Moreover, when coupled with the calling Paul described in Romans 15:14-21, we might hear these words as an invitation to witness and service. Paul trusted in the power of the Spirit to guide his ministry. The one who makes a pool in the wilderness, who brings comfort to the disheartened, is the same one who brings us our good news. Soon, and very soon, all will be healed.

THINK ABOUT

When have you experienced feelings of emptiness?

How many children in your community are exposed to lead in their drinking water? What could you or a group from your church do to respond?

In the busyness of Advent, where do you find stillness?

PRAYER

Loving God, you give us strength, and offer us the richest of blessings. Help us to trust in you, and make our hearts glad at the assurance of coming presence. Amen.

The Eleventh Day Of Advent

Season Of Promise

By Chris Keating

Genesis 15:1-18

> *After these things the word of the Lord came to*
> *Abram in a vision, "Do not be afraid, Abram, I am*
> *your shield; your reward shall be very great." But*
> *Abram said, "O Lord God, what will you give me, for I*
> *continue childless, and the heir of my house is Eliezer*
> *of Damascus?" And Abram said, "You have given me*
> *no offspring, and so a slave born in my house is to be*
> *my heir"* (vs. 3).

IN THE WORD

In a season shaped by pregnancy, Genesis provides a glimpse into the struggles of couples faced with infertility. Like so many in our congregations, Abraham and Sarah have prayed, and prayed, and prayed some more. In their youth, every month brought fresh disappointment. As the years passed, disappointment churned into bitter acceptance. It appeared there would never be grandchildren bouncing on Abraham and Sarah's gnarled knees.

Still, the promise remained.

What makes the situation worse is that Abraham had believed God's promise. It was the promise that had led him out of the homeland. Later, it was the promise that led him to build an altar in the place where the Lord had said his offspring would one day live. Then the promise sent him to Egypt, where Sarah suffered the indignity of being offered as a concubine to Pharaoh. Later the promise led him back to the land of blessing. At this point, Abraham had become a rich man, blessed with gold and livestock. Next the promise led him to the Oaks of Mamre, where God added military commander to his growing "resume". The promise had led him all across the ancient world — but where had it gotten him?

God had promised so much, but as Abraham said, "You have given me no offspring." In response, the Lord said, "Do not be afraid." When Abraham pushed back, God invited him to gaze up into the sky. God gave Abraham a chance to stare up into the heavens. Once more God assured Abraham that a child would be born to him. After all that had happened, Abraham believed. (Sarah was another story. It took her a little bit longer to get on board.)

What led Abraham to believe is impossible to know. But something moved within him. Something changed that night, "and the Lord reckoned it to him as righteousness."

At first, Jesus' words in Matthew may seem to contradict Abraham's stalwart faithfulness. Jesus seemed to indicate that it was actions that lead to our justification, and not faith alone. Yet the contexts are different. Jesus spoke to Pharisees bent on trapping him in heresy; he reminded them that they were nothing but a brood of vipers who had abandoned faithfulness in speech and action. Jesus called the disciples to embrace the sort of vulnerable faith Abraham had embodied — a faith that trusts, even when the night is dark, and the promise has not yet been fully realized. "For out of the abundance of the heart the mouth speaks."

IN THE WORLD

When our daughters were little, we spent many Advent evenings driving around neighborhoods looking at holiday light displays. We lived near Kansas City at the time and would often drive down to the renowned Country Club Plaza to see its astonishing light displays. Looking at the hundreds of thousands of lights strung across the Spanish-themed shopping district was a bit like looking at the blinking lights of countless galaxies. Each night our girls would ask to see the "pretty lights," and off we would go — bundled up a bit like Abraham and Sarah off in pursuit of a promised adventure. When a promise has claimed your heart, you dare to move forward, even when the night is dark.

Advent, like any of God's promises, is much more than a candle dangled in front of our eyes. The days of Advent and the coming of Christmas are more than rewards promised to us for good behavior. At times, our waiting for God's promise may be long. There will be moments of disappointment. The barrenness which weighs heavy on Abraham and Sarah, and so many in our congregations, will be real.

Not everyone will have a child or a grandchild. Not everyone will experience the warming presence of God on a cold night. But listen to the story of Abraham and Sarah and see if you can hear your name being called. Remain faithful, as Jesus adjured. Listen for the words of assurance, "Do not be afraid." Lean forward and dare to trust that the one who has promised is coming.

THINK ABOUT

What practical steps can you take to help those for whom this journey of Advent is filled with barrenness and struggle?

Look out into the night sky, and read Genesis 15:5-6. What words of assurance do you hear?

PRAYER

God, in these long nights of waiting, help me to find comfort in the promise of your coming. Amen.

The Twelfth Day Of Advent

Stranger In A Strange Land
By Chris Keating

Ruth 1:15-17

> *So she said, 'See, your sister-in-law has gone back*
> *to her people and to her gods; return after your sister-*
> *in-law.' But Ruth said, 'Do not press me to leave you or*
> *to turn back from following you! Where you go, I will*
> *go; where you lodge, I will lodge; your people shall be*
> *my people, and your God my God. Where you die, I will*
> *die — there will I be buried. May the Lord do thus and*
> *so to me, and more as well, if even death parts me from*
> *you!'*

IN THE WORD
It's clear from the beginning of Ruth's story that she was a woman who knew how to get things done. Her story was told with eagerness and hope, and was filled with the images of turning and reversal. Kathleen A. Robertson Farmer noted that within its compact 84 verses, the book of Ruth used the Hebrew word for "turn" or "go back" fifteen times, including twelve times in chapter one. The repeated use works to keep readers on the edge of their seats, telegraphing the theological message of redemption found throughout Ruth. It's clear something big is about to happen, just as it is for us in Advent.

Other word clues offer insights into the story's use of ironic images, including plays on the expression of "fullness" and "emptiness." Displaced from Bethlehem because of a famine, Elimelech, an Ephrathite (from the root "fruitful" or "productive") and his family settle in Moab. Their search for abundance eventually led to even deeper emptiness, however, when Elimelech and his sons Mahlon and Chilion all died. Verse five captures the tension well: "both Mahlon and Chilion also died, so that the woman was left without her two sons and her husband."

No wonder Naomi described her life as turning from fullness to emptiness, from sweetness to bitterness (1:20-21). Having heard that times have changed, Naomi turns back to Bethlehem. After a while, she suggests that her daughters-in-law return to Moab. It's probably for the best, given that most Israelites held Moabites in contempt. She pushed them to do the sensible thing: cut their losses, return home, and get on with life.

Naomi offered the women her blessing and kissed them goodbye. With some prodding Orpah headed back to Moab, but Ruth clung to her mother-in-law. She embodied the sort of *hesed* (loving kindness) which God offered to God's people. She remained steadfast in offering a love that (literally) would not let go. It's important to note that instead of seeing this as a choice forced on Ruth or dictated by others, this is a counter-cultural decision. By the same token, Orpah should not be condemned for returning home. Both women acted with faithful courage.

While we read Ruth's words as "I will go" and "I will lodge," in Hebrew the sentence has no verbs. Instead of communicating a future reality, Ruth was stating a plain in-the-moment fact: "your God, my God; your people, my people." Ruth had committed herself to the ways of Yahweh.

For Ruth, there was no turning back. She moved forward, perhaps caught on the idea that something good might just happen in Bethlehem after all.

IN THE WORLD

The plain truth of the matter is that Ruth was a vulnerable young immigrant, a widowed refugee headed to a nation where she would be a hated minority. Further, she lacked any visible means of support. Like refugees of every time and place, she would be subject to a political system she may not have fully understood. She would be thrown into an economic system in which she had few, if any, privileges. The odds were not in her favor, a harsh reality faced by many immigrants today. Despite this, Ruth chose to stay with her mother-in-law. It was a choice made in love.

Her story reminds us that there are real people in the middle of our heated political debates over immigration. On a good day, refugees face difficulties few of us can imagine. Their lives are often filled with bitterness and emptiness. Having fled homelands out of fear, they are left in places without many options. It is not an easy way — but still they cling to the idea that something wonderful may soon happen.

Years ago, a nurse in our congregation was volunteering at a clinic when she met a refugee family from Burundi. She began speaking to the father. In very limited English, he told her they had just arrived from a United Nations refugee camp, landing in the United States in the middle of winter without shoes or coats. Within weeks they were expected to enroll their children in school, find an apartment, get jobs, and begin repaying the standard refugee resettlement loan offered by the United States.

And they did. Like Ruth, they clung to each other and to a dream. Like Ruth, they were foreigners in a foreign (and often, hostile) environment. It drives home the importance of the *hesed*-love we offer to each other. As a refugee, Ruth knew that kindness was the best choice she could make, which was perhaps the most valuable lesson for us this Advent.

THINK ABOUT

Where are ways you can minister to refugees or immigrants this Advent?

How could "turning" find its way into your Advent vocabulary?

Would you be able to share even a simple act of loving kindness to someone today?

PRAYER

Loving Lord, we live by faith and the expectation that, in you, the future is always open and filled with possibilities. Walk with us, God, as we enter each new day and fill us with that sense of hope and love that filled Ruth when she stood with Naomi and headed toward Bethlehem. Amen.

The Thirteenth Day Of Advent

Jesus' Family Tree
By Thomas C. Willadsen

Ruth 4:13-17

> *So Boaz took Ruth and she became his wife. When they came together, the Lord made her conceive, and she bore a son. Then the women said to Naomi, "Blessed be the Lord, who has not left you this day without next-of-kin; and may his name be renowned in Israel! He shall be to you a restorer of life and a nourisher of your old age; for your daughter-in-law who loves you, who is more to you than seven sons, has borne him." Then Naomi took the child and laid him in her bosom, and became his nurse. The women of the neighborhood gave him a name, saying, "A son has been born to Naomi." They named him Obed; he became the father of Jesse, the father of David.*

IN THE WORD

Today's reading is the happy ending of the book of Ruth. It is a significant text to consider during Advent, because the baby born to Ruth and Boaz would become the grandfather of David. As we are less than two weeks from celebrating the birth of the Christ in the City of David, it is a good time to consider Jesus' genealogy.

The book of Ruth is an elegant novella. Its action is compact and suspenseful; today's reading is as close to "happily ever after" as one can find in the Bible.

The story begins with three women, a mother-in-law, Naomi,and her daughters-in-law, Orpah and Ruth, becoming widows. Naomi decided to return to Judah, her native land. One daughter-in-law, Orpah, remained in Moab. The other daughter-in-law, Ruth, decided to stay with Naomi. Naomi was against Ruth's returning with her at first, but when she saw how determined Ruth was Naomi dropped the discussion.

At the end of the first chapter, when Naomi returned, Bethlehem was buzzing like a beehive. Naomi told the welcoming committee to call her "Mara," that is, "bitter," rather than her given name, Naomi, which means "pleasant," or "nice." She told them "the Lord has dealt bitterly with me."

In the second chapter, Ruth went to glean barley that the harvesters had dropped. Her hard work got the attention of Boaz, the owner of the field she had been gleaning in. Boaz sent Ruth home to Naomi with extra grain, in addition to what she had gleaned.

Naomi cleverly instructed Ruth how to get Boaz's attention on the evening when he winnowed the harvest, and maybe got a little tipsy celebrating, and went to sleep in the garner. The action was mysterious there in the dark, but Ruth showed that she was available for marriage and was a virtuous woman. Boaz sent her home with a lot of grain again.

In the final chapter, Boaz accosted the one man in Bethlehem with the right to redeem the land of Ruth and Naomi's late husbands, thus also acquiring Ruth herself. When the man declined to redeem the land, Boaz redeemed it. Boaz and Ruth married and had a son... which brings you to today's reading. Naomi was restored. The child was placed in her bosom; Naomi became his nurse. The women of Bethlehem gave the baby the name Obed. Obed was the father of Jesse and Jesse was the father of David.

If you take a look at the genealogy that comes in the first chapter of the gospel of Matthew, only four women are mentioned:

Tamar who masqueraded as a prostitute so that her father-in-law, Judah would provide her with a son; Rahab, the prostitute who hid the spies Joshua sent to view the land near Jericho; Ruth, the first convert to Judaism; and "the wife of Uriah" as the gospel names her; her given name was Bathsheba.

The women named among Jesus' ancestors were all outsiders. While Jesus was "from the house and family of David," there are some notorious people mixed in as well.

IN THE WORLD

People who are into genealogy know that it is the stories that are hidden that are the most interesting. The stories of the horse thieves are much more interesting several generations later than those of nobility. The women mentioned as ancestors show us that the Lord works through ordinary and profoundly human people "his wonders to perform."

THINK ABOUT

Has God ever gotten your attention, taken you by surprise, using someone you did not expect to bring you a message of faith?

Has God ever gotten through to you any other way?

PRAYER

Living God, you created all people in your image. Give us the patience and wisdom to see you in everyone we meet. In Jesus' name we pray. Amen.

The Fourteenth Day Of Advent

Exalted And Humbled
By Thomas C. Willadsen

1 Samuel 2:1-8

> *Hannah prayed and said, "My heart exults in the Lord; my strength is exalted in my God. My mouth derides my enemies, because I rejoice in my victory. There is no Holy One like the Lord, no one besides you; there is no Rock like our God. Talk no more so very proudly, let not arrogance come from your mouth; for the Lord is a God of knowledge, and by him actions are weighed. The bows of the mighty are broken, but the feeble gird on strength. Those who were full have hired themselves out for bread, but those who were hungry are fat with spoil. The barren has borne seven, but she who has many children is forlorn. The Lord kills and brings to life; he brings down to Sheol and raises up. The Lord makes poor and makes rich; he brings low, he also exalts. He raises up the poor from the dust; he lifts the needy from the ash heap, to make them sit with princes and inherit a seat of honor. For the pillars of the earth are the Lord's, and on them he has set the world."*

IN THE WORD

Today's reading is Hannah's Song. Tomorrow's reading will be The Magnificat, the song of praise that Mary sang immediately after greeting Elizabeth. The songs are very similar, though the women's circumstances were different. Hannah was rejoicing in her pregnancy. A year earlier she had visited Shiloh and poured out her heart in prayer because she desperately wanted a child. Her husband Elkanah's other wife, Peninnah, had given him numerous children. Peninnah was mean to Hannah. Even though Hannah was Elkanah's preferred wife, Hannah still wanted a child of her own.

She presented herself to the Lord, weeping. She prayed silently, but her lips were moving, so Eli, the priest, assumed she was drunk. Hannah corrected this assumption and said she was pouring out her soul in prayer. Then Eli answered, "Go in peace; the God of Israel will grant the petition you have made to him."

Today's reading is the song of praise Hannah raised at Shiloh when we she dedicated her son, Samuel, to the Lord's service there.

IN THE WORLD
Hannah prayed a prayer filled with reversals for the world she lived in. Currently in the United States the gap between rich and poor is the largest it has been for generations. While unemployment is also at historic lows, many people are having to work multiple jobs to provide for their families. Some people are having to choose between buying food and buying prescription drugs. *USA Today* recently reported the death of a woman in Kentucky who had cut back from the recommended dose of insulin because she could not afford what she needed. This is only one example of how difficult and perilous it is to be poor in our nation.

Hannah's prayer was based in her own sense of vindication, but she expressed a desire for her society to be turned upside down.

We're approaching the Christmas season. There are numerous drives to see that poor children receive toys and poor families can have feasts, at least on Christmas day. In my own community, the shelters have no trouble at all finding people to provide and staff the evening meal. They always serve "turkey with all the trimmings." There will be an evening meal the day after Christmas. Often, the guests who enjoyed the traditional feast the day before do not have any way to store the leftovers that many believe are the best part of the holiday.

Two days a year, "those who were hungry are fat with spoil." Yet there is no safe, warm place to go on days when the public library is closed.

THINK ABOUT

Who are the "fat cats" who should be brought down from their high status places in 2019?

Do you know anyone who is poor, who lives in the dust whom the Lord will exalt?

When have you been humiliated, abased or brought down a peg? What did you learn from that experience?

When have you been vindicated and had your social status restored?

PRAYER

Creator God, each Sunday we sing that from you "all blessings flow." Give us the vision to see the people in our community who need to receive the blessings of safe places to live and not fear that they will not have enough to eat. Give us the courage to speak out against injustice. Give us the compassion to see that all people have been made in your image. Give us grace to accept grace. Guide our words and actions by your Spirit to use the gifts you have given us, gifts of energy, intelligence, imagination and love to lift up the lovely. We pray in Christ's name. Amen.

The Fifteenth Day Of Advent

The Road Home

By Thomas C. Willadsen

Isaiah 35:1-10

> *The wilderness and the dry land shall be glad, the
> desert shall rejoice and blossom; like the crocus it shall
> blossom abundantly, and rejoice with joy and singing.
> The glory of Lebanon shall be given to it, the majesty
> of Carmel and Sharon. They shall see the glory of the
> Lord, the majesty of our God. Strengthen the weak
> hands, and make firm the feeble knees. Say to those who
> are of a fearful heart, "Be strong, do not fear! Here is
> your God. He will come with vengeance, with terrible
> recompense. He will come and save you." Then the eyes
> of the blind shall be opened, and the ears of the deaf
> unstopped; then the lame shall leap like a deer, and
> the tongue of the speechless sing for joy. For waters
> shall break forth in the wilderness, and streams in the
> desert; the burning sand shall become a pool, and the
> thirsty ground springs of water; the haunt of jackals
> shall become a swamp, the grass shall become reeds
> and rushes. A highway shall be there, and it shall be
> called the Holy Way; the unclean shall not travel on it,
> but it shall be for God's people; no traveler, not even
> fools, shall go astray. No lion shall be there, nor shall
> any ravenous beast come up on it; they shall not be
> found there, but the redeemed shall walk there. And the
> ransomed of the Lord shall return, and come to Zion
> with singing; everlasting joy shall be upon their heads;
> they shall obtain joy and gladness, and sorrow and
> sighing shall flee away.*

IN THE WORD

The prophet foretold amazing reversals. The desert would be filled with flowers. The blind would see; the deaf would hear. The unsteady would stand strong. The very strength of the Lord would restore the people. Everyone would be safe. Everyone would be safe on the highway that leads home.

IN THE WORLD

Isaiah did not just promise a road in today's reading. The road that would lead the people home was a highway. In the United States we might imagine a stretch of interstate (or "an I road," as I grew up calling them). Our interstate highway system is amazing. It began in the Department of Defense to help people and cargo to move quickly in the event of war. The roads were carefully designed. At least one out of every five miles has to be straight, so airplanes can land on them in emergencies.

We often lose sight of the significance of their being "high" ways. In this case "high" means something like "public" or "open to all." We speak of the high seas in the same sense.

The best feature of the holy highway, in my opinion is, "no traveler, not even fools, shall go astray." I have a dreadful sense of direction. I literally need to follow the exit signs out of public restrooms. Whenever I am travelling with someone else to a place we have never been before, I assume they have a better idea of which way to go. This was a major problem the afternoon I learned that my older son had inherited my bad sense of direction. We were unable to successfully return to the highway we had just gotten off of in route to my cousin's house. All we had to do was reverse the route we had taken ten minutes before. We stopped counting wrong turns when we hit eight. We found ourselves in completely unfamiliar parts of the city he had attended college in for three years. It got so bad we stopped and asked for directions.

I have never feared lions attacking me on the road, though once a deer crashed into my car. I have never been blind, or deaf, or suffered from weak knees, but I have gotten lost - epically lost - many times.

I imagine the highway Isaiah described. The scenery would be gorgeous. Abundant water would transform a barren place, filling it with flowers. Everyone on it would be singing happily, and no one, not even me, would get lost. Hallelujah.

But the best part is that this safe, beautiful, foolproof highway would lead us home.

THINK ABOUT

Where is the Holy Spirit leading you?
What makes you think you're on the right path?
How does it feel when a sign tells you to change course?

PRAYER

Lord of all, in this season of preparation, open our eyes, our ears, and our hearts to recognize your presence in our lives, pointing our way, leading us, recalculating our paths, and guiding us home. We pray in the name of the risen Christ. Amen.

The Sixteenth Day Of Advent

Hope
By Thomas C. Willadsen

Psalm 42

> *As a deer longs for flowing streams, so my soul
> longs for you, O God. My soul thirsts for God, for the
> living God. When shall I come and behold the face of
> God? My tears have been my food day and night, while
> people say to me continually, "Where is your God?"
> These things I remember, as I pour out my soul: how
> I went with the throng, and led them in procession
> to the house of God, with glad shouts and songs of
> thanksgiving, a multitude keeping festival. Why are
> you cast down, O my soul, and why are you disquieted
> within me? Hope in God; for I shall again praise him,
> my help and my God. My soul is cast down within me;
> therefore I remember you from the land of Jordan and
> of Hermon, from Mount Mizar. Deep calls to deep at
> the thunder of your cataracts; all your waves and your
> billows have gone over me. By day the Lord commands
> his steadfast love, and at night his song is with me, a
> prayer to the God of my life. I say to God, my rock,
> "Why have you forgotten me? Why must I walk about
> mournfully because the enemy oppresses me?" As with
> a deadly wound in my body, my adversaries taunt me,
> while they say to me continually, "Where is your God?"
> Why are you cast down, O my soul, and why are you
> disquieted within me? Hope in God; for I shall again
> praise him, my help and my God.*

IN THE WORD

The psalmist is talking to herself. In the midst of a time of struggle and fear, she is seeking a message of hope. In a time of drought, salted with her tears, she expresses the need for refreshing, cool water. There is rhythm of hope and despair, security and abandonment.

Many who have experienced a dark night of the soul report that the Lord is nearest when one feels the most isolated. Perhaps the fierce longing is itself precisely what is best. As Thomas Merton expressed, "But I believe that the desire to please You, does in fact please you." The psalm ends on a note of hope, without denying the sadness and isolation; hope remains.

At this time of year, you might hear a modern version of Psalm 42, Merle Haggard's Christmas classic, "If We Make It Through December." This was Merle Haggard's lone Top 40 pop hit. It also charted on Billboard's County and Christmas harts in 1973. Haggard sings of the difficulty of being laid off and the sadness he feels in not being able to provide "Christmas here" for his little girl.

Like the psalm, the song ends with a hope, repeating the song's title with "we'll be fine."

IN THE WORLD

Sometimes, when I begin to speak to a crowd, I ask the audience to raise their hands if they ever talk to themselves. Generally, around half of the crowd raises their hands. The fun comes in watching the faces of those who have not raised their hands. They have a puzzled look and whisper, "Do I talk to myself? Well, I guess, maybe once in a while..." Laughing at ourselves and realizing that everyone talks to themselves brings crowds together. My uncle adds that sometimes he has to talk to himself, when he needs an expert opinion. Do not go to this man for instruction in humility.

In the past two decades churches have begun offering Blue Christmas worship. For many people Christmas is not a time of joy and celebration, but a time of deep sadness and loneliness. Families facing their first holiday season since the death of a loved one often find it hard to celebrate; things just seem off-kilter. Recalling happier times can make the contrast with the present sadness all the sharper.

One response to the sadness that sometimes comes in this season is to find other people who feel equally out of step with the happiness that they imagine surrounds them. Another is to lean into the memories, as the psalmist does, recalling happier days in the festivals at the temple.

THINK ABOUT

When have you felt God's absence?

When you long to feel the presence of God, the way a desert desires rain, do you spend time in silence, listening, waiting?

How do you experience hope when you are discouraged? Is being discouraged the same for you as being hopeless?

PRAYER

Nurturing, protecting God, I lift my heart to you, confident of your great love for all of creation. Speak to me in silence. Give me a heart eager to embrace the hope you send with each new day. I lift this prayer to you in the name of your son, Jesus the Christ. Amen.

The Seventeenth Day Of Advent

Remember Who You Are; Remember Whose You Are

By Thomas C. Willadsen

Jude 1:17-25

> *But you, beloved, must remember the predictions of*
> *the apostles of our Lord Jesus Christ; for they said to*
> *you, "In the last time there will be scoffers, indulging*
> *their own ungodly lusts." It is these worldly people,*
> *devoid of the Spirit, who are causing divisions. But you,*
> *beloved, build yourselves up on your most holy faith;*
> *pray in the Holy Spirit; keep yourselves in the love*
> *of God; look forward to the mercy of our Lord Jesus*
> *Christ that leads to eternal life. And have mercy on*
> *some who are wavering; save others by snatching them*
> *out of the fire; and have mercy on still others with fear,*
> *hating even the tunic defiled by their bodies. Now to*
> *him who is able to keep you from falling, and to make*
> *you stand without blemish in the presence of his glory*
> *with rejoicing, to the only God our Savior, through*
> *Jesus Christ our Lord, be glory, majesty, power, and*
> *authority, before all time and now and forever. Amen.*

IN THE WORD

Last summer I led a class called "The Bible for People with
Short Attention Spans." In five one-hour classes we read six
books in their entirety. There is a lot to gain from studying these
overlooked gems like Jude often is. Go ahead, read the whole

book, not just the verses above; I'll wait for you here. Later today tell someone you read a book — start to finish — before breakfast.

One of the strange things about Christians is that we read other people's mail. A good portion of what we call the New Testament is correspondence among Christians when the church was just getting started.

Jude wrote to a group of Christians to remind them of the faith that brought them together and brought them to Christ. Some outsiders, scoffers, grumblers, and malcontents were trying to get them to turn from following the true faith. Jude advises the Christians to show mercy to those who are in error, reminding them of the security of dwelling in God's love.

Take the last two verses of this reading with you today. These words soar. These words keep us from falling. These words remind us of God's relentless love for all people.

IN THE WORLD

Pundits say that American society has never been more polarized than it is right now. (Actually, I'm writing this in March, but I doubt the situation will have changed much by the day you are reading it.) It's hard to know when and how to engage people whose views are different from one's own, because some of us get really passionate. In times like this it is often best to slow down and simply remember who we are. Jude suggested that those with a strong, though not rigid, identity in Christ, can withstand having their faith assailed. He even advised Christians to extend mercy to others. After all, God started this whole mercy business by the grace of Christ. Don't forget that.

THINK ABOUT

When your faith is weak, how do you strengthen it?

What factors in your life make it difficult to live your faith every day?

How does it feel when someone extends mercy to you?

How does it feel to extend mercy to someone else?

Today, do something kind for someone who will never know you did it.

PRAYER

Lord of all, lead my heart to accept your acceptance. Remind me of the mercy and grace with which you embrace the world. As the celebration of the birth of your son nears, startle me again with the miracle of your word made flesh. I lift this prayer to you in his name. Amen.

The Eighteenth Day Of Advent

Restored, At Last
By Thomas C. Willadsen

Zechariah 8:1-17

*The word of the Lord of hosts came to me, saying:
Thus says the Lord of hosts: I am jealous for Zion with
great jealousy, and I am jealous for her with great
wrath. Thus says the Lord: I will return to Zion, and
will dwell in the midst of Jerusalem; Jerusalem shall be
called the faithful city, and the mountain of the Lord of
hosts shall be called the holy mountain. Thus says the
Lord of hosts: Old men and old women shall again sit in
the streets of Jerusalem, each with staff in hand because
of their great age. And the streets of the city shall be
full of boys and girls playing in its streets. Thus says
the Lord of hosts: Even though it seems impossible to
the remnant of this people in these days, should it also
seem impossible to me, says the Lord of hosts? Thus
says the Lord of hosts: I will save my people from the
east country and from the west country; and I will bring
them to live in Jerusalem. They shall be my people and
I will be their God, in faithfulness and in righteousness.
Thus says the Lord of hosts: Let your hands be strong
— you that have recently been hearing these words from
the mouths of the prophets who were present when the
foundation was laid for the rebuilding of the temple, the
house of the Lord of hosts. For before those days there
were no wages for people or for animals, nor was there
any safety from the foe for those who went out or came*

*in, and I set them all against one another. But now I will
not deal with the remnant of this people as in the former
days, says the Lord of hosts. For there shall be a sowing
of peace; the vine shall yield its fruit, the ground shall
give its produce, and the skies shall give their dew; and
I will cause the remnant of this people to possess all
these things. Just as you have been a cursing among
the nations, O house of Judah and house of Israel, so
I will save you and you shall be a blessing. Do not be
afraid, but let your hands be strong. For thus says the
Lord of hosts: Just as I purposed to bring disaster upon
you, when your ancestors provoked me to wrath, and
I did not relent, says the Lord of hosts, so again I have
purposed in these days to do good to Jerusalem and
to the house of Judah; do not be afraid. These are the
things that you shall do: Speak the truth to one another,
render in your gates judgments that are true and make
for peace, do not devise evil in your hearts against one
another, and love no false oath; for all these are things
that I hate, says the Lord.*

IN THE WORD

Today's reading is exceptionally long. It looks ahead to a
time of restoration, a return from exile. The reading feels almost
nostalgic. For people in twenty-first century America, the idea of
old people sitting in the streets and playful children running in
the streets feels like an idyllic vision of a former time, Mayberry
in 1961. The Lord, through the prophet, is promising peace and
security.

IN THE WORLD

The prophetic words we find in the Hebrew scriptures are
not glimpses of what the future holds. Rather, they show the
consequences of neglecting justice and not protecting the poor
and vulnerable. Tell the truth, they say to us. Have a fair judicial
system. Keep your promises.

In a year and a half, my state will be drawing new legislative districts. This has always been a contentious issue. Today it is more contentious because our knowledge of who lives where is very precise. It is tempting for the party that was out of power at the last redistricting to get revenge, to draw the new districts to favor their election. There are some people, on both sides of the aisle, who see that both parties, and all people, suffer when districts are not equitably configured. Perhaps next time we will find a way for every vote to have an impact. It would help us render "judgments that are true and make for peace."

THINK ABOUT

When you were twelve years old how did you feel when a situation was unfair?

Now that you're (your age here____) how do you feel when a situation is unfair?

Besides old people sitting on park benches and children playing outside, what would be signs of a harmonious community to you?

PRAYER

God of Shalom, our hearts are restless, our minds are easily distracted. Lead us to the peace you desire for creation, peace that is more than the absence of war. Guide our hands and feet to work for justice and equity. Give us room in our hearts and nation to welcome all your children. We pray in the name of the Prince of Peace. Amen.

The Nineteenth Day Of Advent

Glamping In The Cedars
By Bethany Peerbolte

Samuel 7:9-10

> *I have been with you wherever you went, and have*
> *cut off all your enemies from before you; and I will*
> *make for you a great name, like the name of the great*
> *ones of the earth. And I will appoint a place for my*
> *people Israel and will plant them, so that they may*
> *live in their own place, and be disturbed no more; and*
> *evildoers shall afflict them no more.*

IN THE WORD

David was feeling guilty that he had built himself a comfortable and strong home, but God was still housed in an old raggedy tent out back. His generous solution was to plan an extravagant home for God. A home that had physical walls that were strong and would stand the test of time. David wanted God to enjoy all the modern amenities that he enjoyed, maybe a little so he felt less guilty for having them himself. Even though God's prophet, Nathan, said God was all for this idea, in reality, a stationary home was not in God's plan.

God pointed out to Nathan that God never asked for a house, but God knew David meant well and approved the project. Nathan was instructed to tell David that God was making a great home for him, for David. God built David a home without physical walls but still one that was strong and would stand the test of time. The house God built was in David's bloodline and would stand the test of time because God was committed to

David's family. David thought that the epitome of luxury was a home made of cedar but God showed that there was more value in being God's family.

IN THE WORLD

For years I have been jealous of a camping weekend a group of my friends go on. The stories from their weekend together are constantly retold throughout the winter months and rekindle their hope that summer will come again. They are the one group of people I interact with that never complain about the winter. Every time someone begins to complain, another person instinctively tells a story from their camping adventures. I have strategically inquired and enthusiastically marveled at their stories and this year... I was invited!

Plans began to be hashed out in January, dates were chosen, campsites booked, and then the packing list went out. I knew immediately I had made a terrible mistake. My understanding of camping was obviously very different from theirs. I was expecting a campsite with hook ups for electricity, real restrooms, and showers nearby. The packing list had things on it like "portable shower" and "poop shovel."

I was in over my head. I do not actually like camping, I like sleeping in a tent and waking up to modern amenities (500 yards away max). However, at this point, I had put so much into getting the invitation I couldn't bring myself to back out. Their inspiring stories still stand and I wanted that for me. I wanted to be a part of their connection and commitment to hope during the drab winter months in Michigan.

David wanted my kind of camping. He wanted as many conveniences as he could get as close as he could get them. Of course, David was willing to invite God on the "glamping" trip, too! God, however, was more committed to connecting to people. Sure, God could do that in a fancy temple, and God agreed to have a temple built, but the real work would be done among the people. God would endure the air-conditioned temple, and I suppose I would endure learning how to use a poop shovel. The conveniences God planned for David, however, were to be built within God's people and would be a legacy of hope and blessing for the world.

THINK ABOUT

What assumptions have you made about God? How have you built God into a temple and hindered God from moving freely in your life? Is there an inconvenience God is asking you to endure in order to build God's family?

PRAYER

Accommodating God, I want what you want, but sometimes I get distracted by the easy path. Help me choose building of family over building of temples. Thank you for enduring my assumptions and gently nudging me back to the legacy you want for my life. Amen.

The Twentieth Day Of Advent

The Bread Of Tears

By Mary Austin

Psalm 80:1-7, 17-19

> *O LORD God of hosts, how long will you be angry*
> *with your people's prayers? You have fed them with*
> *the bread of tears, and given them tears to drink in full*
> *measure* (vs. 4-5).

IN THE WORD

"The bread of tears" is such a vivid image that we know right away what the psalmist meant. Each of us has experienced the kind of grief where everything we eat tastes like tears. We open the fridge, and nothing seems appealing, but we know we have to eat. Advent offers us a respite from eating our tears. Advent channels our grief toward God's vision of the future. We are invited to lift up our heads and consider the kind of universe that God intends for humankind.

IN THE WORLD

One of my enduring memories is of my mother-in-law, before she was my mother-in-law. My husband-to-be and I had traveled to the south to visit his parents because his father was ill. Looking back, I can see that my father-in-law knew he was dying before anyone else did. As I sat with him in the evening, he started to sing "I'll Fly Away." In the night, as I slept on his floor, I could hear his breathing change, and in the morning, he slipped away.

Once she learned that her husband of fifty years was gone, my soon-to-be mother-in-law sat at the breakfast table, eating a bowl of cereal so she could take her medication. She didn't make a sound, she just cried silently as she ate the food she needed so she could take her pills. Tears ran down her face, and into her cereal bowl, and her breakfast that day was a meal of cereal and salty tears.

Advent offers us hope beyond those tear-filled meals that life brings to all of us. For these four weeks, we get to see beyond sorrow to a transforming joy, and to take in the promise of God's strength for all of our challenges. The Lord, the God of hosts, weeps with us, and shows us a world beyond tears.

THINK ABOUT

When have you dined on tears? How did your tears or those of another change the flavor of the food you ate? In America we have a tradition of bringing food to the home of a bereaved family. How does this image of "the bread of tears" affect your understanding of that custom?

PRAYER

Holy God, we know that you look at the world and weep, as we do. We trust that you see our tears, and, when they are our food, day and night, that your care also sustains us. Turn toward us, we pray, and meet our sorrow with your promise of peace. In the name of the Christ child, Amen.

The Twenty-First Day Of Advent

Waiting... And Waiting

By Mary Austin

Galatians 4:4-7

> *But when the fullness of time had come, God sent his Son, born of a woman, born under the law, in order to redeem those who were under the law, so that we might receive adoption as children. And because you are children, God has sent the Spirit of his Son into our hearts, crying, 'Abba! Father!' So you are no longer a slave but a child, and if a child then also an heir, through God.*

IN THE WORD

As we wait for Jesus to come, the apostle Paul reminds us that we have been made children of God. We call on a God who is not remote or disinterested, but who is as close as family. We are related to God by adoption, meaning that we are chosen by God to be part of the family. We know that we carry the divine DNA, as we are made in the image of God, and now we are adopted. We carry a double relatedness to God, by our very birth and by God's choice. Both layers are at work in our lives.

IN THE WORLD

Some years ago, friends decided to adopt a baby, and all of their circle of friends became interested in the process. We watched them make their adoption book (this was before the digital age) where they showed pictures of themselves, their home, and their pets, and tried to show why they would be the ideal parents for someone's baby. In the book, they each wrote about why they wanted to be parents, and the kind of life they had to offer a baby.

Eventually a young woman who knew she was too young to be a good mother chose them to adopt her son. That baby is in high school now, and has had a whole different life because his parents longed for him, prayed for him, and waited for him, and because his birth mother chose them to be the parents for her son. The adoption process revealed love – and pain – on all sides.

They prepared more deeply to be parents than many people who give birth to children, and the time of waiting was much longer than nine months. If God adopts us as part of the divine family, we can imagine God preparing for us, and waiting for us, until we're finally part of the family. In Advent, as we anticipate the coming of Jesus, we can remember that God has waited for us, too.

THINK ABOUT

Advent is, as much as anything, a time of waiting. Think back about something for which you waited… and waited… and waited, wondering if the required time would ever pass. Why is it that waiting for something seems to make it all the more precious when it finally arrives?

PRAYER

God of love, we come in awe that we are both born into your family and chosen by you in our adoption as your children. We relish our double layer of belonging, and come to you as your grateful people. In Jesus' name, Amen.

The Twenty-Second Day Of Advent

Even Not Deciding Is Deciding
By Mary Austin

Matthew 1:18-25

> *Now the birth of Jesus the Messiah took place in this way. When his mother Mary had been engaged to Joseph, but before they lived together, she was found to be with child from the Holy Spirit. Her husband Joseph, being a righteous man and unwilling to expose her to public disgrace, planned to dismiss her quietly. But just when he had resolved to do this, an angel of the Lord appeared to him in a dream and said, "Joseph, son of David, do not be afraid to take Mary as your wife, for the child conceived in her is from the Holy Spirit. She will bear a son, and you are to name him Jesus, for he will save his people from their sins." All this took place to fulfill what had been spoken by the Lord through the prophet: 'Look, the virgin shall conceive and bear a son, and they shall name him Emmanuel', which means, 'God is with us.' When Joseph awoke from sleep, he did as the angel of the Lord commanded him; he took her as his wife, but had no marital relations with her until she had borne a son; and he named him Jesus.*

IN THE WORD
A lot of anguish is summed up in the words "planned to dismiss her quietly." The story says that Joseph had resolved to do this, suggesting a long process. Perhaps he had nights of tossing and turning, trying to make this decision, and days where

it was hard to concentrate on his work because of the thoughts that flooded his mind. Still, even in his embarrassment and confusion, Joseph wanted to dismiss Mary quietly.

At that point, God sent an angel in a dream to reassure Joseph. One wonders why God didn't spare him all that anguish, and clue him in from the beginning. For Joseph, and for us, the process of making a decision is as important as the decision itself. The time we spend thinking, weighing options, praying for help, and listening for wisdom shapes our lives as much as the decision itself does. Making the decision is part of our spirit's formation.

IN THE WORLD

"Did you go to visit a bunch of colleges when you were in high school?" a friend asked me recently, as she was traveling around taking her child to visit potential universities. It's a rite of spring break for people of means, visiting colleges with high school students, so the students can think about where they want to apply.

It's a nice bonding time for parents and kids, which may be why people like to do it. Under no other circumstances would a teenager choose to spend the entire spring break with their parents.

Often, in winter, it's the season of waiting for acceptance letters, and scholarship news. The heady days of spring, when every college seemed like a possibility, are over. But the truth is, for most kids, most colleges will be fine. This is their first big, life-changing decision, and almost every school will teach the essentials: how to run your own life, how to get along with other people, how to let go of judgments about how others live, and how to know your own mind instead of going with the crowd. But in the visits, and the pondering, the student learns a lot about herself. The process of being trusted with a big decision develops skills we all need later.

Making the decision about college, or work, or the military is part of the process of growing up. For us, too, making hard choices is part of growing into God's presence.

THINK ABOUT

What are some hard choices you had to make? What process did you use to come to your decision? Whom did you consult? What resources did you bring into the process?

In what way was the process as important as the decision, itself?

What difficult decisions, if any, do you face this Advent season? What process will you use to make them?

PRAYER

God of dreams and visions, God of angel messengers and the deepest wisdom, we thank you for your presence with us as we wrestle with difficult choices. Form us into your people, as we seek the right path. In Jesus' name, Amen.

The Twenty-Third Day Of Advent

Enough Is Enough

By Mary Austin

Galatians 3:6-14

> *"For all who rely on the works of the law are under a curse..."* (vs. 10)

IN THE WORD

As part of his long exhortation to the churches in Galatia, Paul was reminding them that following the old law was no longer necessary, now that there was direct access to God through the life and work of Jesus. But grace doesn't feel like enough to them; the people of the Galatian church felt an anxious need to do something more to assure their closeness to God.

We are subject to the same temptation. We want to add something on to the gift of grace, by making sure we're doing enough Bible reading, enough serving in the world, enough giving. Grace is great, but it never feels complete, and so we're tempted to add more.

IN THE WORLD

In these last days before Christmas, these are a powerful words.

This is God's word of peace to anyone who is lamenting that the Christmas Eve bulletin isn't quite perfect, or that the church doesn't look updated enough for the guests who will make their semi-annual appearance. This is God's word of peace to anyone who is frantically baking cookies, or cleaning before a family dinner. This is God's word of peace to anyone who feels like they haven't prepared enough for Christmas. There's always one more tweak to the sermon, one more practice that the kids need for the pageant, one more check of the candles. There's always another side dish to make, another gift to buy, another card to write.

"Enough," God says.

My enduring memory of Christmas as a child is of my mother being stressed and anxious. I'm sure she was working hard to create wonderful memories for us. There were well-chosen, age-appropriate gifts that she and my dad assembled late in the night on Christmas Eve. A delicious Christmas dinner was always served. But my strongest memory is of her mounting tension as she never felt like she had done enough. It was a relief when Christmas was over. As an adult, I do very few things for Christmas, and my biggest aim is to enjoy the people. I turn down holiday events that I don't think will be fun, or if there are too many things in a week, I pare down. I have noticed that the bakery makes excellent cookies and pies. The church looks good enough, and typos in the bulletin creep in, in spite of all the proofreading. My hope is just to savor the journey of Advent, and the awe of Christmas.

We have done enough. We are enough.

The coming of the Christ child seals that for us, and we are invited to put away our lists and our expectations of ourselves, and take in God's gift.

THINK ABOUT

What are the worries, the stresses, the fears, and the anxieties that threaten to undo Christmas for you? What would it take for you to let go of those things and walk away from them so you can walk, worry free, into the stable at Bethlehem?

PRAYER

Loving God, teach us again that enough is enough. We praise you for the gift of the Christ child, who brings your presence to us and to the world. Help us to stop, and receive the gift of that grace, free from the need to do anything to add to it. In the name of the Prince of Peace, Amen.

Nativity Of Our Lord

Our Story

By Mary Austin

Luke 2:1-7

> *In those days a decree went out from Emperor*
> *Augustus that all the world should be registered. This*
> *was the first registration and was taken while Quirinius*
> *was governor of Syria. All went to their own towns*
> *to be registered. Joseph also went from the town of*
> *Nazareth in Galilee to Judea, to the city of David called*
> *Bethlehem, because he was descended from the house*
> *and family of David. He went to be registered with*
> *Mary, to whom he was engaged and who was expecting*
> *a child. While they were there, the time came for her*
> *to deliver her child. And she gave birth to her firstborn*
> *son and wrapped him in bands of cloth, and laid him in*
> *a manger, because there was no place for them in the*
> *inn.*

IN THE WORD

Almost every Christmas Eve, we read this story as part of our Christmas celebration, and we know it as well as we know any story in the Bible. We know how quickly the story moves from the powerful, as Caesar Augustus issued his order for a census, to the insignificant parents-to-be, Mary and Joseph. They were just two people among the thousands coming to be counted. We know how quickly the story tells of Jesus' actual birth, and then moves to people even lower on the social scale. We know the familiar contours of the story, as the shepherds woke up in those chilly fields to find the light of God's angelic messengers all around them.

Still, there are some surprises... From top to bottom, the whole world is turned upside down on this night. Ordinary, unnamed parents, counted by Rome only for taxation, have given birth to God's miraculous child. The angels come to earth to announce it not to kings and rulers, but to shepherds.

The story is filled with people who shouldn't be there. Only the men of the household needed to be counted for the census. Joseph could have gone without Mary, made much better time and had a much easier journey. And those shepherds, out in the fields — the good news came first to the shepherds, dirty and disreputable people, way out in the fields. Why announce such a miraculous birth to such scruffy, unreliable people? Luke meant for us to understand from the very beginning that this good news is for everyone, for all of God's people, from the least to the greatest. Luke wanted us to know from the beginning that this birth is announced to people like us, so we, too, can take in this good news.

IN THE WORLD

The presence of all these characters in the story reminds us that there is always a place for us in God's story. Whether we come to church every week, or only under duress. Whether we live exemplary lives, or are barely hanging on. Whether we feel like we know God, or whether we're just getting started. If there's room for shepherds and a carpenter and an unmarried mother, there's a place for us, too.

To find the child of God born in a stable reminds us again that God is everywhere, certainly among the powerful, but even more so among the lost, the cold, and those who are far from home.

Surely, this night God is with us, but also on the heating grates of Detroit, in the refugee tents around the world and among the travelers stranded in airports. In the feeding stations of Somalia and the gardens of stone at Arlington Cemetery. This is God's story, and it is also our story. We have a place in it, right next to the stable and the smelly shepherds, standing with the bewildered parents and the triumphant angels. We belong in this story like no other, and God has made a place for us.

THINK ABOUT

Picture the traditional nativity scene in your mind. Now place yourself within the scene. Where are you standing or sitting? Why?

PRAYER

God of all times and places, God of all who love you, we fall to our knees today in awe at the place you make for us in the story of the Christ Child. May we, too, draw near and worship him, filled with your transforming gifts of hope and promise. In Jesus' name, Amen.

The Nativity Of Our Lord

Let It Go
By Mary Austin

Luke 2:8-20

In that region there were shepherds living in the fields, keeping watch over their flock by night. Then an angel of the Lord stood before them, and the glory of the Lord shone around them, and they were terrified. But the angel said to them, "Do not be afraid; for see — I am bringing you good news of great joy for all the people: to you is born this day in the city of David a Savior, who is the Messiah, the Lord. This will be a sign for you: you will find a child wrapped in bands of cloth and lying in a manger." And suddenly there was with the angel a multitude of the heavenly host, praising God and saying, "Glory to God in the highest heaven, and on earth peace among those whom he favors!" When the angels had left them and gone into heaven, the shepherds said to one another, "Let us go now to Bethlehem and see this thing that has taken place, which the Lord has made known to us." So they went with haste and found Mary and Joseph, and the child lying in the manger. When they saw this, they made known what had been told them about this child; and all who heard it were amazed at what the shepherds told them. But Mary treasured all these words and pondered them in her heart. The shepherds returned, glorifying and praising God for all they had heard and seen, as it had been told them.

IN THE WORD

The Christmas story is so familiar that we don't realize there's an incredible moment of suspense in it – a moment when the whole story can move forward, or fall apart. It all turns on one moment in the story.

It all hinged on the shepherds. It's great that that baby was born... that the angel came... but the whole thing depended on that moment when the shepherds looked at each other, and decided what to do. We can imagine them wondering if they should leave their sheep, and go see this baby... or wait and see what other people do. Were they being punked? Did they imagine the whole thing? If anything happened to their sheep, they were responsible for the whole value of the sheep. It's an early version of "you break it, you bought it." You lose it, you pay for it. No doubt one of them is urging caution. "Let's stay here," you can imagine him saying, "we have no idea what's going on out there." But others urged them to go and see.

The message of the angels turned out to be so compelling that they looked at each other, and decided to leave to go see that new baby. They were willing to leave their work and their responsibilities to go and see.

IN THE WORLD

The whole story hinges on us, too. If there's no one to tell the story, no one knew about this gift of God's presence in the world. To tell it, the shepherds took a big risk. Like them, there are risks for us, too. There are things we have to let go of, to make room.

We all have something we have to leave behind to take in the wonder of the Christ Child. It might be a persistent feeling that things are always going to go wrong... or deep doubt about our own talents... or a big pile of rage at how someone has treated us. It might be the feeling that if we stop grieving for someone, we're disloyal. Or the feeling that we should be able to do it all ourselves. Maybe we work too much, or yell too much, or shop too much. Maybe the *Real Housewives* on TV are more compelling than our real neighbors.

We all have something to leave behind, so we can meet up with the Christ child. We have to pare down... let go... leave things behind... so there's room in the inn of our hearts for God.

THINK ABOUT
What do you need to let go of, to leave behind, so you can fully appreciate and accept Jesus Christ into your life?

PRAYER
Along with the glorious angels and the lowly shepherds, O God, make us your messengers. We pray that our lives would show your goodness, and our actions tell your story. At each place of risk, may we take up the courage of the shepherds and the light of the angels, and tell your story in all that we are and do. In the name of the wonderful counselor, mighty God, Prince of Peace, Amen.

The First Day After Christmas

A Phrase Of Praise

By Bethany Peerbolte

Psalm 148: 10-13

> *Wild animals and all cattle, creeping things and*
> *flying birds! Kings of the earth and all peoples, princes*
> *and all rulers of the earth! Young men and women*
> *alike, old and young together! Let them praise the name*
> *of the Lord, for his name alone is exalted; his glory is*
> *above earth and heaven.*

IN THE WORD

This psalm has one purpose: praise. The expanse of the praise is exhausting. Humans praise from high born to low, all genders, all ages, all humanity is called on to praise God. Creation praises from sun to moon, all animals, all plants, all of creation is called on the praise God. This praise is bookended by "hallelujah." Praise the Lord! It's a simple enough psalm and its energy is undeniable.

IN THE WORLD

This seems like a cruel verse to study the day after one of the highest energy holidays of the year. Almost as cruel as requiring one to immediately box up all the Christmas decorations. I am one of those people who leaves decorations up until Epiphany, not because I have a deep-rooted commitment to the church calendar, but because I am lazy. For me the tradition of Boxing Day seems cruel.

I have just spent weeks preparing. I have carefully unearthed and lugged containers of decorations from the basement. Painstakingly chose each piece of décor's perfect location. I have woken up early to get the best deals on the best presents. I have waited in line with cranky customers. I have planned and executed an absurd number of recipes. I have been pleasant at family gatherings and grateful for every gift given to me. I do *not* want to spend the very next day cleaning and packing away all that is Christmas. I simply do not have the energy.

This psalm, however, does have the energy. This psalm reminds me of a prayer I heard my niece pray once where she rattled off every noun she could think of to be thankful for. With a delicious smelling meal right under our noses the prayer felt like an eternity to get through. When my niece finished her endless thanksgiving prayer, we were all doubly thankful for the meal of which we were about to partake.

If you have no more energy, praise is a good way to refuel. This psalmist literally looked around and saw all the praise that surrounded them. The trees, the sun, the animals, the kings, and the old; they were all shouting praise to God. If you find yourself saying "oh God" today make it a phrase of praise.

THINK ABOUT
Take a moment to look around; what to your left is giving praise to God? To your right? In front of you? Beneath you? Above you? Within you?

PRAYER
God of every moment, in this moment let me give you praise. Even when I do not feel like praising, let the things around me make up for my lack. You are worthy of praise and praise will be my goal today. Amen.

The Second Day After Christmas

Therefore, Get Wisdom
By Bethany Peerbolte

Proverbs 8: 22-31

> *The Lord created me at the beginning of his work,*
> *the first of his acts of long ago. Ages ago I was set up,*
> *at the first, before the beginning of the earth.* (vs. 22-23)

IN THE WORD

Wisdom was pleading her case for why humanity should value her. In the verses preceding these, she had pointed out that through her the kings rule and her wealth was incomparable to human riches. She continued her case by comparing her position with that of any firstborn. Firstborn children have a special place in the families of her audience. The firstborn is given special blessings, and a greater share of the inheritance. When the head of the house is gone, they are the default leader. Wisdom was reminding Israel that before God began creating, God sought out wisdom. She had been a part of all creation from the beginning and was a good resource to tap into.

IN THE WORLD

"Wisdom is the principal thing; therefore get wisdom" (Proverbs 4:7).

"To be successful, find someone who has achieved your dream and ask them how they did it." I can't remember where I first heard these words of wisdom or if it was in a book, a mentor, a daydream; I have no recollection. No matter, they have been great words of advice. I have met incredibly inspiring people because of these wise words.

Essentially, these words encourage us to seek a mentor who is at a place in life or career that we wish to be. They urge us to listen to the wisdom they have picked up along the way. Seeking help is not always as easy as it seems. We hear stories of singularly unique pioneers creating a new industry on their own and we think we can do it alone too. We are inspired by stories like the life of Walt Disney, who created new worlds from his own imagination.

If God prioritizes wisdom, then we should too. Wisdom is stored in the collective experiences of the people around us. It may seem like Walt Disney blazed a new trail and started a new industry, but even Walt had mentors. When a new idea popped into his head, he trusted the reactions of his daughters. When he wanted to create a theme park, he studied other parks and carnivals learning from their successes and failures. Even when we are off in our own world, wisdom is all around us.

Seeking her input first is righteous and godly work.

THINK ABOUT

What goals do you have? How have you or could you put the pursuit of wisdom first in achieving those goals? Verses 30-31 say wisdom is playful like a child; how have you included play and imagination in your goal setting?

PRAYER

God, you acquired wisdom before you began creating, putting wisdom before all else. As I work with you to create your kingdom on earth, send me wisdom. Always keep wisdom in front of me and let it be the guiding light for my path. Amen.

The Third Day After Christmas

Millstones And Stumbling Blocks
By Bethany Peerbolte

Matthew 18:1-14

> *"If any of you put a stumbling block before one of these little ones who believe in me, it would be better for you if a great millstone were fastened around your neck and you were drowned in the depth of the sea.* (vs. 6)

IN THE WORD
Jesus was enjoying time with his followers when the disciples asked "which one of us is the greatest?" Jesus called a child over, placed her in the middle of the men, and said, "This child is the most valuable member of God's kingdom. The children do not seek to be anything but what they are, and that humility makes them the greatest." Jesus then went on to explain that anyone who messes with childlike humility has a terrible fate ahead of them. A fate that will make a person wish for a slow death by drowning than to receive what they deserve. Jesus advises to not be a stumbling block in someone's faith.

IN THE WORLD
There is a moment in our lives where pride tells us to lie about our achievements. That moment must come sometime after first grade.

"I'm the fourth best spitter in my class!" That is how Caleb greeted me on Sunday morning.

I bent down to get more information. I asked Caleb how he knew he was the fourth best spitter in his class. Obviously, there had been a contest and I was the silly one for not knowing that right away. Caleb told me all about the contest and how close he had gotten to third place. He also told me in great detail how amazing of a spitter Greg was and how Greg was the best by far.

This is the humility of a child. Caleb didn't exaggerate and say he was third, even though he had come really close to third place. Caleb didn't complain about the wind or find another excuse for his fourth-place placement. Caleb was proud of who he was, the fourth best spitter in his class. Pride had not yet taken hold of Caleb or taught him to lie, exaggerate, or explain away who he is.

Jesus condemns all who place stumbling blocks in the path of childlike humility. While there are times when other people create stumbling blocks in our lives, often we create the stumbling blocks ourselves. We compare our accomplishments to others'. We adhere to expectations that if we thought about them we don't really want for our lives. We feel like we need to exaggerate what we have accomplished to look successful on social media. A child does not seek to be anything but what they are, and that is the key to citizenship in God's kingdom.

THINK ABOUT

Is there something you have oversold, or discredited because you didn't value it enough? What would it be like to be proud of the smaller accomplishments? What would it be like to not beat yourself up about a failure? How else are you creating stumbling blocks in your own life (negative talk, procrastination)?

PRAYER

God, you are great. As I seek to be more like you, help me to remember to be humble. When I am in fourth place help me be proud of who I am and be happy for those ahead of me. Let me notice when I place a stumbling block in my own path, so that I may walk unhindered on the path you call me to. Amen.

The Fourth Day After Christmas

Into The Good Place
By Bethany Peerbolte

Hebrews 2:10-18

> *For it is clear that he did not come to help angels,
> but the descendants of Abraham. Therefore, he had to
> become like his brothers and sisters in every respect, so
> that he might be a merciful and faithful high priest in
> the service of God, to make a sacrifice of atonement for
> the sins of the people* (vs. 16-17)

IN THE WORD

The opening of this section of scripture identified Jesus as "archegos" of glory, or the pioneer of glory. This word is most often used to recognize someone as the head or founder of something. Someone who is an "archegos" is the origin of something meant to attract other participants. Jesus is the founder of a family meant to welcome in new brothers and sisters. The writer was rejecting the view that God is detached from the world. In fact, God wants to be a part of creation and to establish a family that will share God's blessings with the world. Jesus is the founder of that vision and that family.

IN THE WORLD

The Good Place is a comedy series on NBC about four people who get sent to hell but they think they made it into heaven. Demons set up an elaborate town of torture to drive the humans crazy for eternity. In season three, the theology of this show developed into an intriguing examination of what it really means to be "good" versus "bad," and a recent episode (S3 E11) ran parallel to what the writer of Hebrews explaining. To really understand humanity, one must get down here and see for one's self.

In the show, there is an accounting system in which individuals can gain or lose points based on their actions. One of the demons, who has befriended the main human characters, finds out no one has gotten into heaven for 500 years. He presents this issue to the judge whose initial reaction is to back up the status quo, "rules are rules." After some thought however, she decides to pop down to earth to see for herself. She is gone for all of 5 seconds before she comes back and understands the problem. In her words "OH brother! That was rough! Earth is a mess, y'all, WOOF." Next season we get to see how her advocacy will help sort out the bad accounting and what the new system will be.

Those of us who have read the Bible know the best part is coming. The part of the story where the judge begins a new operating system and more people are invited into "the good place." Jesus came to earth to understand the problem firsthand. He was a great pioneer because he started by becoming like those he wanted to help. The greatest leaders are the ones who seek to understand the plight of the lowest members of their organization. They don't run from the dirty or tedious work, they dive right in.

Jesus became one of us "brothers and sisters" living in creation. He relates to our plight because he has lived it and felt it. He didn't come to pound old teachings into our heads or shove the "right" way in our faces. He walked alongside us, as us, to offer another way to live life.

THINK ABOUT

Is there someone you know needs help? Have you made yourself like them to better understand their plight? How does having a pioneer like Jesus help you walk in your faith? What system of grace and glory do you advocate for?

PRAYER

God of glory, you came into the dirt of this world to help us. The world could have continued with the old accounting, but you wanted more for us. Thank you for pioneering a new family. Help me to see through the eyes of my sisters and brothers so that I can see life from the same angle you do.

The Fifth Day After Christmas

Praying, Planning, And Giving

By Bethany Peerbolte

Psalm 20

> *The Lord answer you in the day of trouble! The*
> *name of the God of Jacob protect you!* (vs. 1)
> *May he grant you your heart's desire, and fulfill all*
> *your plans.* (vs. 4)
> *Some take pride in chariots, and some in horses, but*
> *our pride is in the name of the Lord our God.* (vs. 7)

IN THE WORD

Psalm 20 can be broken into three sections. The first section is about what God will do simply because God is God. God has promised to protect and support. The next section is about what the faithful have done to show their trust in God; give offerings, plan, and pray. The final section is assured that the victory is already won because the faithful have trusted and God has kept all promises.

IN THE WORLD

The relationship presented in this psalm may just rival the steamy romance in Song of Solomon. One partner keeps all their promises, and the other partner offers back tokens and gestures of their affection. It's a perfect relationship.

This give and give relationship is not often the way we see our relationship with God. Usually we focus on how God has all the power, and that God does not need us. Any therapist worth their hourly fee would flag a relationship like that as unhealthy. This psalm pulls us back into a healthier way of being in relationship with God. It is a way that recognizes our role.

Our role is to give offerings. We need to recognize the gifts we have in abundance and find ways to use them to advance our relationship with God. God gives good gifts. We should use them and not let them gather dust at the back of the closet.

Our role is to make plans. Plans show our intent and what we are willing to do to reach a goal. Inevitably it will be up to God if the plans play out, but if we never plan God has nothing to work with.

Our role is to pray. Our prayers show God where our priorities and passions are leading. Certainly, God knows what needs to be done, but having support of one's partner helps make the work more meaningful and fulfilling.

THINK ABOUT

What role have you neglected (offering, planning, praying) in your relationship with God? How has God shown commitment to your relationship? Has there been a time when you found God was simply waiting for you to offer, plan, or pray?

PRAYER

Faithful God, we make a good team. Even when I have ignored my role, you have always been there to protect and support me. Together we will achieve the victory and in all times, I will give you the glory. Amen.

The Sixth Day After Christmas
(New Year's Eve)

Who Are You?

By George Reed

John 8:12-19

> *Again Jesus spoke to them, saying, "I am the light*
> *of the world. Whoever follows me will never walk*
> *in darkness but will have the light of life." Then the*
> *Pharisees said to him, "You are testifying on your own*
> *behalf; your testimony is not valid." Jesus answered,*
> *"Even if I testify on my own behalf, my testimony*
> *is valid because I know where I have come from*
> *and where I am going, but you do not know where I*
> *come from or where I am going. You judge by human*
> *standards; I judge no one. Yet even if I do judge, my*
> *judgment is valid; for it is not I alone who judge, but*
> *I and the Father who sent me. In your law it is written*
> *that the testimony of two witnesses is valid. I testify on*
> *my own behalf, and the Father who sent me testifies*
> *on my behalf." Then they said to him, "Where is your*
> *Father?" Jesus answered, "You know neither me nor*
> *my Father. If you knew me, you would know my Father*
> *also."*

IN THE WORD

Jesus was defining himself for the people. He knew who he was and was willing to share that knowledge with others. Not all of the others were thrilled with what he said.

IN THE WORLD

People often ask us who we are. It may come out as "Don't I know you?" or "Who do you think you are?" Sometimes we ask ourselves the question. There are so many ways to answer a question like this. We can talk about our family tree with its nationalities and ethnic groups. We can talk about our hometown and where we grew up. We can talk about our education and training. We talk about being employed or working in our home. We can talk about our family and any children we may have. There are so many ways to identify who we are.

All of these ways are valid and can be helpful to people who want to know about us or even to help us understand ourselves. But our best bet is to follow the lead of Jesus. Jesus defined himself by his relationship to God and the task that God had assigned to him. He understood himself as a child of God. Jesus is the light of the world because he knows his Father is light. He knows he is the son of the great king.

There are many who would put us down because we may not belong to the 'proper' groups. We may not agree with them on politics or religion. Our skin color may be different from theirs. Our country of origin, however long ago our ancestors came here, is not the same place that they, our critics, came from. It may be financial differences or just personalities that don't match. People are always ready to judge. Again, the example of Jesus shows us the way: If we know who we are, we don't need to judge others.

We are also children of God. We were created in the likeness of our Creator and, as Jesus taught us, we are also the light of the world. We are children of the most high king. We have nothing to be ashamed of and we have nothing to prove. We are God's children and God's light to the world. We have no need to judge others because we know who we are and it is more than enough. We do not need to judge others because they are also God's children however different they may be from us.

The light of the world has come into our world and shown us that we are light, as well.

THINK ABOUT

Who am I? Where do I take my cues for defining myself? Do I define myself as God defines me, a child of God and the light of the world?

PRAYER

O God who is light and blessing: Grant us the grace to identify ourselves as your children and as a source of light for our sisters and brothers. Amen.

The Seventh Day After Christmas
(New Year's Day)

Now More Division
By George Reed

Revelation 21:1-6

> *Then I saw a new heaven and a new earth; for the first heaven and the first earth had passed away, and the sea was no more. And I saw the holy city, the new Jerusalem, coming down out of heaven from God, prepared as a bride adorned for her husband. And I heard a loud voice from the throne saying, "See, the home of God is among mortals. He will dwell with them as their God; they will be his peoples, and God himself will be with them; he will wipe every tear from their eyes. Death will be no more; mourning and crying and pain will be no more, for the first things have passed away." And the one who was seated on the throne said, "See, I am making all things new." Also he said, "Write this, for these words are trustworthy and true." Then he said to me, "It is done! I am the Alpha and the Omega, the beginning and the end. To the thirsty I will give water as a gift from the spring of the water of life".*

IN THE WORD

This scripture seems far removed from Christmas at first glance but it speaks so beautifully of what must have been in Jesus' mind when he told us that the kingdom of God is within us. For God to reign in us means that heaven has indeed come

123

down to earth. God's presence is here among us. The sea, the waters of chaos that would destroy God's good creation, is no more. There is no separation of heaven and earth.

IN THE WORLD

There seems to be so much division in our world. As much as we talk about peace on earth and goodwill to all at the Christmas season, we do not experience it so much as talk about it. Christmas can be a time when we feel most deeply those who are missing from our lives either because of death or estrangement. It can be a lonely and frustrating time. Even for those do not find it so, it can be such a hectic time that we really don't make the time to spend in deep conversation and relationships.

While social media takes a probably deserved slap because we spend so much time on our devices that we ignore those around us, it also has been a means whereby I have reconnected with folks that I have not seen in a long time. When I get a friend request from someone from my recent or distant past, it brightens my day. Often these people are physically far removed from me and it is not practical for me to see them in person but we still get to make a connection.

There are also those people that are near enough that I could be in contact with but I do not make the time to really sit down and talk with them. My brother and I are busy with our careers and we live a good distance away so we only see each other once or so a year. Recently I have had the opportunity to take a workshop near his home. He graciously offered to let me stay with him and his wife. It has been a wonderful time. We don't have a lot of time to just sit and talk but it is precious time. I am reminded of the joy I miss on a daily basis because I don't make the time to share deeply with other people.

The scripture today reminds us that God's deep desire is to be with us and for us to be with each other.

THINK ABOUT

Who do you need to connect or reconnect with? Who is right around you that you need to spend time with? Does God figure into that?

PRAYER

O God who is community within your own self: Grant us the wisdom to make the time to be in communion with you and with one another. Amen.

The Eighth Day After Christmas

Being Sure
By George Reed

Hebrews 11:1-3

> *Now faith is the assurance of things hoped for,*
> *the conviction of things not seen. Indeed, by faith our*
> *ancestors received approval. By faith we understand*
> *that the worlds were prepared by the word of God, so*
> *that what is seen was made from things that are not*
> *visible.*

IN THE WORD
The scripture speaks about faith as something very concrete. This is not about wishful thinking; this is about how we ground our lives in what is real. It is not the things that we see that are real and the unseen which is questionable but the other way around because the visible was created out of the invisible. It is the spiritual realm which holds reality and it is to that realm we are called.

IN THE WORLD
There does not seem to be much that we can be sure of in this world. I grew up near Dayton, Ohio, where National Cash Register (NCR) was a huge employer. The campus of the company was made up of several blocks of multi-storied buildings. The company not only had an international school for training people but their own hotel to house them when they came to town.

That is now all gone from Dayton.

I am writing this in Saginaw, Michigan, just north of Flint and Detroit, which were once bustling with the energy and wealth of the auto industry. It is where once busy auto plants were teeming with workers and there are now empty lots. It is where hardworking people once lived and now there are abandoned homes or overgrown lots.

None of this is news. Most of us have experienced it firsthand and we are not the first to find that the things we thought were the very foundation of our culture have gone away. Whether it was technological change, a potato blight, the plague, or devastating storms the ways things were has changed for people throughout time.

And yet there is a permanence offered to us. It is the sure knowing that God is with us in all the changes of life. And it is not that our faith expressions don't change. We sing different songs in worship and we use different metaphors to talk about the deep things of faith. Our knowledge of language and culture has grown. That has helped us understand more about the scriptures that we turn to for comfort and guidance. But the rock of our faith is steadfast - Emmanuel, God with us.

Regardless of how things change around us and even with us, we know that we are not alone. There is a presence of love that encompasses us and gives us life. It gives us not just air in our lungs and blood pumping through our hearts, it gives us peace and joy beyond all understanding. It gives us meaning and purpose for our lives as we reach out in love to others.

Faith is not wishful thinking. It is a sure knowing that God is with us, always has been, always will be.

THINK ABOUT

What are some of the things you have seen change in your lifetime? How have you changed? What have you kept through your life journey?

PRAYER

O God who is eternal: Grant us the faith that knows that the deep truths of life and eternity are ever present and ever here for us. Amen.

The Ninth Day After Christmas

A Blessing For The Earth
By George Reed

Genesis 28:10-15

> *Jacob left Beer-sheba and went toward Haran. He came to a certain place and stayed there for the night, because the sun had set. Taking one of the stones of the place, he put it under his head and lay down in that place. And he dreamed that there was a ladder set up on the earth, the top of it reaching to heaven; and the angels of God were ascending and descending on it. And the Lord stood beside him and said, "I am the Lord, the God of Abraham your father and the God of Isaac; the land on which you lie I will give to you and to your offspring; and your offspring shall be like the dust of the earth, and you shall spread abroad to the west and to the east and to the north and to the south; and all the families of the earth shall be blessed in you and in your offspring. Know that I am with you and will keep you wherever you go, and will bring you back to this land; for I will not leave you until I have done what I have promised you."*

IN THE WORD
In his dream, Jacob had a revelation about God and about himself. He discovered that God had not only been with his ancestors but that God promised to be with him. God had rich blessings in store for Jacob but he also will be a blessing to all

the families of the earth. God blessed Jacob so that Jacob could bless others. Nothing has changed through the centuries. God is still with us to bless us so that we can, in turn, bless others.

IN THE WORLD

As I was entering a store the other day two gentlemen were exiting and I overheard a bit of their conversation. The first fellow mentioned that a car that had just driven by was burning a lot of oil and the other fellow responded about how he remembered driving cars like that and was glad those days were over. I could relate and I think all of us appreciate the good things we have. It is no fun when we are struggling and trying to make ends meet, especially when that means not having enough resources to take care of our basic needs.

God created the world with lots of resources. There is an abundance of food, materials and beauty for us to all share. I don't believe that God desires us to be without the necessities of life. I think God wants us to enjoy the things around us. But they are not there to be worshiped. They are not there so we can gather them for ourselves when we already have enough. We have plenty of evidence around us of greed and poverty. As we celebrate the gift of God in Jesus this season, perhaps we can also celebrate his concern for the poor around him by sharing with the poor around us.

THINK ABOUT

Do I/we have more than what I need to take care of my basic needs? If I do, how can I use that so it is a blessing for others as well as for myself? Do I see those around me as part of God's family and therefore as part of mine?

PRAYER

O God who is love and blessing: Grant us the grace to accept your blessings and to share them with whomever we encounter. Amen.

The Tenth Day After Christmas

Standing On Holy Ground

By George Reed

Exodus 3:1-5

> *Moses was keeping the flock of his father-in-law*
> *Jethro, the priest of Midian; he led his flock beyond*
> *the wilderness, and came to Horeb, the mountain of*
> *God. There the angel of the Lord appeared to him in a*
> *flame of fire out of a bush; he looked, and the bush was*
> *blazing, yet it was not consumed. Then Moses said, "I*
> *must turn aside and look at this great sight, and see why*
> *the bush is not burned up." When the Lord saw that*
> *he had turned aside to see, God called to him out of*
> *the bush, "Moses, Moses!" And he said, "Here I am."*
> *Then he said, "Come no closer! Remove the sandals*
> *from your feet, for the place on which you are standing*
> *is holy ground."*

IN THE WORD

This is a familiar passage for most of us when Moses encountered God in the burning bush. It seems like an ordinary day and then Moses noticed that something was different. He went to explore it and met up with God.

IN THE WORLD

Lots of ordinary things are probably going on in most of our lives. We have made it through Christmas Day and New Year's Day and those of us with children are looking forward to school starting and a return to whatever passes for normalcy.

We may think we are finished with Christmas but Christmas is not finished with us! There are still two days of Christmas left. Things may look like they are getting back to normal but God's normal is not the same as ours. God's normal is about coming to seek us, embrace us and call us to new life.

We may not encounter burning bushes or see the skies torn apart today but that does not mean that God is not coming to us. The question is whether or not we are willing to explore what is around us and see what is really happening. It may be a chance encounter at the grocery where we find ourselves searching a common shelf with someone. They may just be a stranger but they are also a child of God. How do we handle that holy encounter? Perhaps just a smile and maybe a quick word of greeting is all it takes to make it a holy moment for both parties.

At Christmas we celebrate the Incarnation, God becoming one of us; literally this means taking on flesh. Christmas is a very special time of incarnation but it has really been taking place from the beginning. God creates a clay person and then breathes into that form God's own breath, God's own Spirit, God's own life. We were made in the image and likeness of God. We are meant to be God's presence to each other. Not just at Christmas but every day.

THINK ABOUT

How can I be God's presence to someone today? What would happen if I expected my meeting someone today to be an encounter with God?

PRAYER

O God who is the one in whom we live and move and have our being: Grant us the grace to find you in our encounters with one another so that we may celebrate your presence with us daily. Amen.

The Second Sunday Of Christmas

Grace Upon Grace
By George Reed

John 1:5-18

> *The light shines in the darkness, and the darkness did not overcome it. There was a man sent from God, whose name was John. He came as a witness to testify to the light, so that all might believe through him. He himself was not the light, but he came to testify to the light. The true light, which enlightens everyone, was coming into the world. He was in the world, and the world came into being through him; yet the world did not know him. He came to what was his own, and his own people did not accept him. But to all who received him, who believed in his name, he gave power to become children of God, who were born, not of blood or of the will of the flesh or of the will of man, but of God. And the Word became flesh and lived among us, and we have seen his glory, the glory as of a father's only son, full of grace and truth.*
>
> *(John testified to him and cried out, "This was he of whom I said, 'He who comes after me ranks ahead of me because he was before me.'") From his fullness we have all received, grace upon grace. The law indeed was given through Moses; grace and truth came through Jesus Christ. No one has ever seen God. It is God the only Son, who is close to the Father's heart, who has made him known.*

IN THE WORD

In this very beautiful and poetic opening of the gospel according to Saint John, we have a wonderful picture of what we have been celebrating throughout this Christmas season. We celebrate the one who was born among us "full of grace and truth". The passage is just filled with wonderful images of the Christ. But it is also about us. It is about us becoming "children of God"; about us receiving "grace upon grace".

IN THE WORLD

Sometimes the disconnect between Christmas and the reality of our world is so great that they seem to be from two different worlds. And they are. The message of Christmas is about the reality of God being with us and inviting us to a way of life that is based on love, caring, and grace. It is about peace on earth and caring for all humankind. It is about the lion and the lamb lying down together in peace and harmony.

The spirit of the world is about being number one, about grabbing all that we can before someone else gets it, and about seeing to it that we get our own way. In this world power is what determines what is right regardless of how wrong it truly is.

The message of Christmas comes to us in this world and quietly announces that things are going to change. It does not come with armies or big bankrolls but it comes with love and a caring spirit. It does not demand that this world change but states that the change is here and is taking place. The reign of God is among us and the birth of the Christ child is our sign of its coming.

Christmas is a time of deciding which message and which world we want to live in. Is Christmas just a holiday season when we act nice to one another or is it the revolutionary statement that this world is changing and it is changing into God's world?

THINK ABOUT

What do I expect from this Christ child? Do I understand how fundamentally he changes our world? Am I willing to be a part of this change?

PRAYER

O God who created and is yet creating this world: Grant us the courage to stand with the Christ child as your call to a new world and a new way of life. Amen.

About the Authors

Mary Austin is the senior pastor of Gaithersburg Presbyterian Church, a diverse Presbyterian church in the Washington, DC area. She has served churches in New Jersey and Michigan, and also loved being a hospice chaplain. She is the author of *Meeting God at the Mall*, published by CSS. She is a graduate of Princeton Theological Seminary and has served churches in New Jersey and Michigan. Her publications include *Call to Worship*, *Presbyterian Outlook* and *Bereavement* magazines. She is deeply interested in the intersections of faith and everyday life, and in what faith means to people throughout their lives.

Dean Feldmeyer is retired and living high atop beautiful Mt. Repose just outside Cincinnati, Ohio, after serving 40 years as a United Methodist pastor. He now serves as a supply preacher and a full time writer. He is an award-winning author of four novels, three nonfiction books, five plays, and numerous articles, essays, and short stories. In his spare time he enjoys playing golf and bluegrass music, but not at the same time.

Christopher Keating is pastor of Woodlawn Chapel Presbyterian Church in suburban St. Louis, Missouri. He is a graduate of Princeton Theological Seminary and Saint Paul School of Theology and writes regularly for *The Immediate Word* on SermonSuite.com. He is a regular contributor to the *St. Louis' Post-Dispatch's Belief* St. Louis blog and has written for the Church of the Brethren's *Messenger* magazine.

Reverend Bethany Peerbolte recognizes her calling is to make scripture relevant to young Christians, and Christians young at heart. She serves as the associate pastor of youth and mission at First Presbyterian Church in Birmingham, Michigan. Her blog, *Millennial Epistle*, seeks to connect scripture to trending topics and contemporary issues. Bethany's commitment to diversity and inclusion has led her to work with Detroit Pride, The Interfaith Council for Peace & Justice, and the National Black Presbyterian Caucus. Bethany holds a Bachelor of Science degree from Michigan State University and a Master of Divinity degree from Ecumenical Theological Seminary.

George Reed, OSL has served as a minister in the United Methodist church for over thirty years. He holds degrees from Wright State University and United Theological Seminary, both located in Dayton, Ohio. He has also taken graduate studies at the Institute of Formative Spirituality at Duquesne University. After serving various UMC churches in Ohio, George is now serving as the Intentional Interim Senior Pastor at Ada Congregational Church/United Church of Christ in Ada, Michigan. He is a contributor to the *Sermons on the Gospel Readings* series and is the author of three-volume (Cycles A, B, and C) series *Lectionary Worship Aids, Series IX.* George and his wife have three grown children.

Thomas C. Willadsen has been a Presbyterian minister for more than 25 years, serving in Minnesota, Maryland and Wisconsin. He has served *The Cresset*, Valparaiso University's Review of Literature, the Arts and Public Affairs as humorist since 1996. Tom graduated from the high school from which Richard Pryor was expelled. He is the author of *OMG! LOL! Faith and Laughter* published by Gemma Open Door in 2012.

www.ingramcontent.com/pod-product-compliance
Lightning Source LLC
Chambersburg PA
CBHW031321040426
42443CB00005B/169